JACQUELI

Discovering
Heraldry

SHIRE PUBLICATIONS LTD

Set in 9 on 9 point Press Roman medium by Oxford Publishing Services. Printed in Great Britain by C. I. Thomas & Sons (Haverfordwest) Ltd, Press Buildings, Merlins Bridge, Haverfordwest, Dyfed SA61 1XE.

Contents

ACKNOWLEDGEMENTS

The cover design is by Ron Shaddock. The drawings are by Jenny Bush and Dennis Lack. The Royal Arms in England and Scotland are reproduced by gracious permission of Her Majesty the Queen. For permission to refer to illustrations acknowledgement is made to Blandford Press for drawings on pages 74, 77, 79, 80 and 81 from *World Heraldry* by Alexander Volborth, to Thomas Nelson and Sons for the scheme of cadency bordures on page 58 from *A Complete Guide to Heraldry* by A. C. Fox-Davies, and to Frederick Warne Ltd for drawings on pages 8, 11, 56, 59, 65 and 74 from *Boutell's Heraldry*.

The author is greatly indebted to J. P. Brooke-Little, Norroy and Ulster King of Arms, for reading the script and generous help.

Stall plate of Sir Ralph Bassett, 1390, in St George's Chapel, Windsor.

Foreword

In recent years there has been a noticeable upsurge of interest in heraldry. Nearly a dozen local heraldry societies have been formed and are flourishing; the Heralds' Museum at the Tower of London has opened and will be visited by the hundreds of thousands of tourists who flock to the Tower each year; heraldic congresses and exhibitions take place with a regularity which would have been unthinkable thirty years ago and a vast number of books has been written on the subject.

However, with but a few exceptions, many of the books on heraldry which have been published during the past ten years have either been weighty tomes, and so expensive, or else children's books which, excellent though many of them are, do not contain sufficient detailed information to satisfy everyone. I hope and believe that this book will usefully fill a lacuna in current heraldic literature.

It has been written concisely and the author has taken pains at all stages to check her facts; consequently the book is full of accurate information, which sadly cannot be said of every book on heraldry. There are plenty of illustrations, which is always desirable in a book devoted to a subject that is, to a great extent, an art form.

Here heraldry is presented as a jewel of many facets, so giving readers a clear insight into the various fascinations of the subject, enabling and encouraging them to move on to study whatever aspects of heraldry interest them most, having been introduced to such aspects in the wider context of the whole art and science of armory.

I congratulate the author on having written a well balanced work, which I feel certain will provide a splendid introduction to a splendid subject for students of all ages.

March 1980

John Brooke-Little
Norroy and Ulster King of Arms

Sir John Chandos, c. 1425. His arms are displayed on his horse as well as his shield, making him easy to identify at the tournament.

1. Introduction

The status value of a coat of arms is neatly illustrated in *Lorna Doone* by R. D. Blackmore. When King James II asks John Ridd what is his chief ambition he replies: 'Well, my mother always used to think that having been schooled at Tiverton, with thirty marks a year to pay, I was worthy of a coat of arms. And that is what she longs for.'

Thus John Ridd would have achieved the insignia of gentility. He disclaims such a desire himself but goes on to say he could afford to 'support a coat of arms' — he could afford to be a gentleman. When the King adds a bonus by making him 'Sir John Ridd' our hero is confused rather than gratified — he knows how to keep up appearances as a gentleman with a coat of arms but cannot see the use of a knighthood to a yeoman farmer! As an Englishman he knows that a title is not a prerequisite to the bearing of arms.

The elements of gentlemanly (originally knightly) status, individuality and distinction implied by the bearing of a coat of arms have been consistent characteristics of heraldry and key elements in its survival. Every man entitled to a coat of arms is pictorially represented as distinct from any other man: however slight the difference, no other contemporary bears an identical coat.

But there is another factor of paramount importance: arms are hereditary and descend unchanged, on the death of the bearer, to the heir apparent in the male line. Younger sons must add marks of difference to the arms, as must the heir apparent during the lifetime of the bearer, to maintain distinction.

One aspect of the identification implied was the use of arms on seals at a time when most people were illiterate. In some instances the design of the arms was based on seals already used. Seals also provided devices used on the personal badges worn by the retainers and household of the feudal lord, and the badges provided devices for the seals. Some badges had very strong associations with their owners and appear in the arms.

When heraldry began the man himself was part of the picture. At the tournament, where true heraldry seems to have its roots, he carried his shield, distinctively painted, and wore his helm with its crest (perhaps) and his surcoat (coat of arms) marked with personal devices. It was important to be able to distinguish individuals and it seems likely that the organising officials, the heralds, would need to advise knights on suitably distinctive colours and devices for their shields, crests and mantles.

7

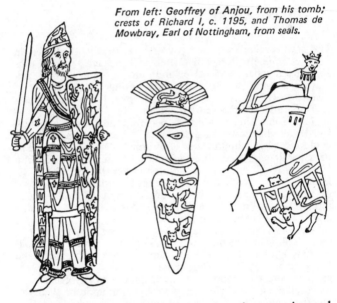

From left: Geoffrey of Anjou, from his tomb; crests of Richard I, c. 1195, and Thomas de Mowbray, Earl of Nottingham, from seals.

The idea was not original; from ancient times warriors and rulers had adopted personal and tribal symbols. The Jews, Greeks and Romans had definite and well established symbols as did many of the barbarian tribes which swept away the Roman Empire. Some of these devices had long associations with families and groups and were incorporated in subsequent heraldic designs, such as the fleur-de-lis of the French kings and the dragon of Wales. But, unlike its antecedents, the phenomenon which developed from the twelfth century set out to be distinctive and was systematised and hereditary. Moreover it was not a gradual development of order in an old haphazard system: heraldry developed very quickly from the first truly heraldic shield of Geoffrey of Anjou in 1127 so that by the end of the century it was an accepted system already formulating the rules and terms which obtain today.

Heraldry appeared almost simultaneously in most countries of western Europe, at a time when knights had regular opportunities to meet knights from other countries, and this seems to be the reason for the unanimity. Earlier writers attributed the main impetus to the crusades, which drew together huge international assemblies of knights to fight for the Holy Land, and identification of groups and individuals must have been very important in the confusion of the progress as well as in battle. Modern opinion, however, inclines to the view that the main incentive was the international character of the tournament in the first half of the twelfth century, anticipating the main crusades. Knights from several countries took part and the tournaments were occasions of great show and pageantry where many individuals had to be distinguished. Furthermore, with the introduction of the closed helm for greater protection, a contestant was unrecognisable except by his trappings.

Thus it seems that through their management of the great medieval sporting and social event the heralds developed a successful system of recognition which was both a science and an art. At first heralds were employed just for the occasion by

*From left, first row: simple coat of **Le Scrope**, a gold bend on a blue field; thirteenth-century banner of the Count of Brittany; Grosvenor, a gold garb on a blue field. Second row: thirteenth-century Duc de Bourbon; fourteenth-century German von Stretlingen; fifteenth-century French seal, Duc de Berri.*

kings and nobles: they proclaimed the event, issued challenges and then organised the proceedings. From their necessary knowledge of armory sprang their initial advisory function and as a safeguard they began to keep records of heraldic arms in Rolls of Arms, many of which survive. Eventually they became permanent household officers and a professional hierarchy emerged. In the fifteenth century they even held conferences.

As feudalism declined with the strengthening of central authority, nobles gradually ceased to employ heralds until only those of the Royal Household remained. The King was able to assert his authority in heraldic matters from the early fifteenth century. The heralds' business was principally with coats of arms, under the authority of the Sovereign through the Earl Marshal, and they made periodic tours of inspection to ensure that arms were being borne correctly by lawful armigers.

From the fourteenth century corporations and prosperous burgesses were joining the ranks of those entitled in chivalry to bear arms: it was as much a mark of honour and standing for a corporation as it was for a successful businessman. Their arms had no functional military role; they were used to dignify

From left: ancient arms of Canterbury; Worshipful Company of the Haberdashers of London; Eton College.

10

and adorn, the secondary role of arms since the beginning. When styles in armour changed during the fifteenth century this secondary role became primary.

The loss of practical purpose had important effects on design. Bold stripes, equilateral divisions, all-over patterns and simple shapes had not long supplied an expanding demand for arms so representations of animals (the royal lion was one of the earliest devices), objects and plants appeared quite early. Many of them became stylised in form or attitude. Reasons for selecting this device or that are sometimes impossible to divine but devices alluding to names — canting devices — were always favoured, for example swine's heads for Hog- or Swyn-.

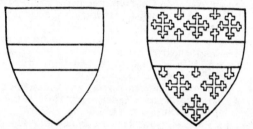

A background of crosses introduced to distinguish branches of Beauchamps.

Within families or feudally connected groups arms had to bear marks of difference and when a man became entitled to more than one coat, through marriage for example, the two coats would be combined on one shield. Simplicity of design was difficult to maintain but, under the restraints imposed by probable display on an actual shield, the heralds maintained an amazing standard. When these restraints disappeared designs gradually became more elaborate and complex, mainly in the effort to represent genealogy. Pictorial devices depicting events or achievements were introduced and the heralds allowed themselves flights of fancy in crests which could never have existed in three dimensions. It required the Victorian romantic passion for medieval studies to lead the reaction against excess and towards designs of less ambition and greater dignity.

Much of modern heraldry derives its standards from the work of medieval heralds. In England and abroad, especially in Scandinavia, it is in civic heraldry that the ancient principles can be combined so well with good modern design. Personal heraldry increasingly inclines to the simplest appropriate design even if it means sacrificing an ancestor or two.

2. Describing the achievement

Armorial bearings are commonly called a *coat of arms* but heraldically speaking this term refers only to the devices borne on the shield. The full display of all the devices to which the *armiger* is entitled by inheritance and personally is an *achievement of arms* or simply an *achievement*.

The central element is the *shield* and it may stand alone. More often, in personal arms, the shield is surmounted by the *helm*, on which is borne the *crest* resting on a *wreath*, *cap of maintenance* or *crest coronet*. *Mantling*, representing protective drapery, flows from the helm and *coronets of rank* (of the peerage and royalty) may be interposed between the helm and the shield. *Supporters*, possibly standing on the *compartment*, may flank the shield. *Personal insignia* may be represented by the circlet with the motto of an order encircling the shield and by badges and medals hanging below. *Mottoes*, not part of the arms officially in England (but they are in Scotland), appear beneath the shield.

Unmarried women, divorced women and widows bear their arms in a diamond-shaped *lozenge*, sometimes surmounted by a lover's knot and without the masculine military trappings. A peeress in her own right has a coronet and supporters. Personal insignia may be displayed.

Terminology

So far most of the terms used, though they may require amplification later, are in understandable modern English; there has been none of the heraldic language which discourages many casual inquirers but which it is necessary to understand to proceed further. It is a minor obstacle, for the terms are easy to learn and pleasant to use. The language of heraldry grew out of the need to record and describe arms in words so accurately that a totally correct picture could be drawn. The early heralds used the Anglo-French of their day in straightforward, economic description. As heraldry expanded new terms came in and a syntax of the order of description was adopted. Some minor changes have been made in recent times but it is generally agreed that the established system conveys an exact meaning succinctly as well as being fundamental to the study of past heraldry.

A verbal description is called a *blazon* and the terms used will be explained as we come to them, which will be in the order of blazoning: components of the shield design, of the crest and the supporters. For convenience arms may be recorded *in trick*, i.e. in outline, with numbers and abbreviations. Uncoloured representations may indicate colour by a system of hatching and dots (less common these days).

TINCTURES

The five colours, three stains, two metals and varieties of fur found in heraldry are called *tinctures* and each has its own heraldic name.

Here the tinctures are indicated by hatching.

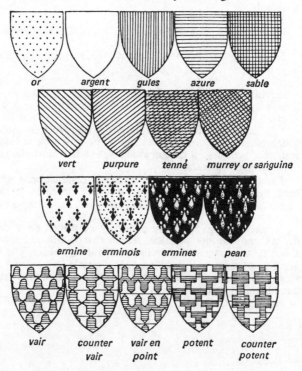

or	*argent*	*gulen*	*azure*	*sable*
vert	*purpure*	*tenné*	*murrey or sanguine*	
ermine	*erminois*	*ermines*	*pean*	
vair	*counter vair*	*vair en point*	*potent*	*counter potent*

13

Colours

Many variations of shade occur within the descriptions and these days particular shades may be indicated in modern terms. Natural or normal colours are described as *proper*, ppr. They are as follows:

Blue, *azure*, abbreviated to *B* or *Az*

Red, *gules,* abbreviated to *Gu*

Black, *sable*, abbreviated to *Sa*

Green, *vert*, abbreviated to *Vt*, *Sin* (Fr)

Purple, *purpure*, abbreviated to *Purp*

The stains were rare until recently, when they have been used more frequently. They are as follows:

Orange tawny, *tenné*

Blood-red, *sanguine*

Purply red, *murrey*

Metals

The two metals are:

Gold, *or* or *gold*, abbreviated to *Or,* usually represented by yellow

Silver, *argent,* abbreviated to *Ar,* usually represented by white

Furs

Ermine spots represent tails, black on white for ermine, the reverse for ermines. Erminois is black on gold; pean is gold on black.

Vair originated from the fur of a certain sort of squirrel which was used to line cloaks. The bluey-grey back and white underside produced a design which was stylised into the form of the original tincture.

There are other much less common combinations which have been used. Combinations of other tinctures in these shapes are called *vairy* of the tinctures used, for example vairy gules and or.

A metal charge may not generally be placed on a metal background for the practical reason that it will not usually show to best advantage, similarly colour on colour. The furs are not so restricted; they may take metals and colours and vice-versa. Exceptions are made to these conventions where good heraldry results.

3. The shield

In theory any shape of shield may be used although today the pointed equilateral form, 2 wide, 3 long, is usually preferred, and this style has always proved most effective for a display of arms. Ancient monuments show many examples of the long tapering shield of the early days and the restrictions it imposed on design. After the shield was abandoned in warfare fanciful shapes with scrollwork appeared but were always less popular in Britain than elsewhere.

Heraldically the shield is described as if by the bearer behind it so that the right-hand side of the drawing is called *sinister* and the left-hand *dexter* (see figure below). The top is called the *chief* and the bottom the *base*. Three points are named for accuracy in positioning: honour (H), fess (F) and nombril (N), as are combinations of the area names, for example sinister base indicates the bottom right-hand section, and centre chief indicates the centre of the top section. The surface of the shield is called the *field*. Anything borne on the field is called a *charge* and anything with a charge on it is said to be *charged*.

Lines of partition

The field can be divided or partitioned in numerous ways, which are described in terms of certain basic geometric charges called *ordinaries*, according to the direction taken by the lines. A *pale*, for example, is a broad vertical stripe down the centre of the shield, so a field divided in two vertically is described as *party per pale* (or *parted palewise*). The tinctures follow, dexter then sinister, thus *per pale argent and gules*. Similarly the field may be party *per fess* (fesswise), *per bend* (bendwise), *per chevron* (chevronwise), *per pall* or *tierced in pairle, per saltire* (saltirewise) and *per cross* or more usually, *quarterly* (page 16).

Varied fields are produced by adding further lines in the same direction, producing an even number of stripes. They are named for the ordinaries again, and the number of stripes is usually given. Thus *paly of six argent and azure* describes a field divided vertically into six stripes alternately argent then azure. Similarly, *bendy, bendy-sinister, chevronny* and *barry* (bar is the diminutive of fess) indicate the appropriate party lines.

Further variations are possible by combining lines of partition and produce some interesting geometric patterns. Paly and barry produce *checky*; bendy and bendy-sinister produce *lozengy* and *fusily* and so on. Per cross and per saltire produce *gyronny of eight* (other numbers may be produced). A single

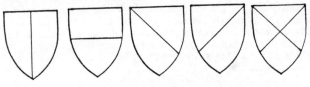

*party
per pale*　　*party
per fess*　　*party
per bend*　　*party per
bend sinister*　　*party
per saltire*

*party
per cross*　　*party per pall
(or tierced in pairle)*

*party per
chevron*

barry   *bendy*   *bendy sinister*   *paly*   *chevronny*

checky   *lozengy*   *fusily*

barry bendy   *paly bendy*   *gyronny*

compony   *counter compony*   *per pale and barry*

ᴗᴗᴗᴗᴗ	engrailed	ՈՈՈՈՈՈ	rayonny
ᴖᴖᴖᴖᴖ	invected	⚜⚜ ⚜⚜ ⚜⚜	floretty
∿∿∿	wavy or undy	⌒	arched or enarched
ᴔᴔᴔᴔᴔᴔ	nebuly	⌒⌒	double arched
∧∧∧∧∧∧	indented	⌐_⌐	angled
∧∧∧∧	dancetty	⟋	bevelled
⊓⊓⊓⊓	embattled	⊓	escartelly
⊓⊓⊓⊓	raguly	⌒	nowy
⊐⊐⊐⊐	dovetailed	⎍⎍	battled embattled
互互互互	potenty	∧∧∧∧∧	urdy
ᴄᴄᴄᴄ	crested	⚜⚜⚜	dancetty floretty

row of chequers is *compony* or *gobony*. Party and varied fields may be combined as in *per pale and barry counterchanged*, where the bars change tincture at the pale line.

So far all lines have been plain but there are numerous ornamental lines which can be used to great effect.

Sometimes an all-over pattern is formed by the regular repetition of a single charge. The field is then said to be *semy* or *poudry* of, for example, horseshoes. Some charges, used often in this way, have special terms. A field of fleurs-de-lis is *semy de lis, fleury* or *floretty*; gold roundels, *bezants*, produce a *bezanty* field; small crosses, *crosslets*, produce a *crusily* field; drops of liquid, *gouttes*, produce a *goutty* field.

18

Decorative patterning known as *diaper* is quite distinct from the effects achieved in partitioning and varying the field. It is introduced to enhance plain areas, often in different shades of the same tincture, and may be in any design so long as it is clearly not a charge or number of charges. It may be in relief and need not conform to the law of tinctures.

chevron engrailed

bars nebuly

per chevron billetty counter changed

bezanty

semy of estoiles

two examples of diaper

19

CHARGES

The honourable ordinaries

The simple broad stripes of colour, some of which gave their names to partitioning lines (see above) are the *honourable* ordinaries, the principal charges blazoned immediately after the field. They are the pale, fess, bend, chevron, cross, *pile*, saltire and, perhaps, the chief and bar. The narrower forms of the charge came to be called *diminutives* and some have distinctive names such as bend — *bendlet*, pale — *pallet*, *endorse*, chevron — *chevronel*. There are usually at least two together. Ordinaries and diminutives may be ornamented and they lie over the field not in it.

chief	*fess*	*pale*	*bend*	*chevron*

pall	*saltire*	*pile*	*cross*

 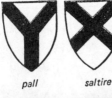

bars	*pallets*	*bendlets*	*chevronels*

fess cotised	*pale endorsed*	*piles*

20

The proportions of the ordinaries and diminutives to the shield have been defined but are not rigid and are secondary to good heraldic design. Thus the chief, fess and pale occupy up to one third of the shield, as do the bend, saltire and cross, unless uncharged, when they occupy one fifth, together with the bar and chevron. The diminutives pallet, bendlet, chevronel and closet are half the width of their ordinaries, the barrulet, endorse and *cotise* one quarter the width.

Where diminutives are used the field must be shown on either side as well as between them to distinguish the charged field from a varied field. The narrowest diminutives are often used to flank their ordinary, which is then described as *cotised* (of the fess, also *closeted*) bend and chevron (also double cotised): the pale is *endorsed*. Charges placed on the ordinaries are vertical except on the bend when they follow the direction of the slope (unless blazoned otherwise). Sometimes charges are grouped along the line an ordinary would take and are described as being *in pale, in fess,* etc. On the

From left: swords in pale, counterpoised fesswise; a pale engrailed between two keys (and) a quill pen palewise; five lozenges conjoined in bend.

other hand, a single charge occupying the position of an ordinary is described as palewise, fesswise etc.

There are said to be over three hundred varieties of cross. The type illustrated with the other ordinaries, where a fess crosses a pale and the links extend to the edges of the shield, is implied by the word 'cross' standing alone. The lines may be ornamental and produce a cross *raguly, indented* etc. Further variations include removing the centre − a cross *voided*, removing the centre quarter − a cross *quarter pierced,* adding a narrow border of a different tincture — a cross *fimbriated*, forming a cross of two endorses and two barrulets interlaced at the centre — a cross *parted and fretty*.

The limbs of the cross may be cut short (a cross *couped*), the simplest of the great variety of crosses which do not extend to the edges of the shield. The Latin, passion or long cross has a long shaft; so does the Calvary cross, which is placed on a given number of steps or degrees, as may be the patriarchal cross, which has its upper limb crossed. The swastika is termed a *cross potent rebated* or a cross *gammadion* or a *fylfot*. Where the limbs of the cross splay out with straight ends it is *formy* or *paty*. The shaft of a cross may taper to a point and this is described as *fitchy*. The Maltese cross is also known as the cross of eight points. The cross of St Anthony or the tau cross has no upper limb and the others are slightly splayed.

The other crosses are largely distinguished by the treatment of the ends of the limbs and some of the commoner examples are illustrated.

The subordinaries

The diminutives are sometimes classed as subordinaries and it matters little so long as the forms are recognised. Neither group is quite so important as the ordinaries.

It is important to distinguish between the charges which follow the shape of the shield around the edges. The *bordure* is a border round the shield and it may be charged, partitioned or treated with ornamental lines. The space it occupies is considerably smaller than that left surrounding a central, shield-shaped *escutcheon*. The *orle* is a narrow bordure following the outline of the shield but set in from the edge and may be ornamental in outline and charged. The diminutive of the orle is the *tressure*, which is nearly always found double and most often *flory counter-flory*, with the heads of fleurs-de-lis alternating on the inner and outer edges and the centre space void. Charges bordering the shield along the line of an orle are said to be *in orle*.

The *canton* is now smaller than a quarter and appears in dexter chief unless blazoned sinister. A *gyron* is now the left triangular section of a canton. Rarely is either form treated with ornamental lines.

The diamond-shaped *fusil* is a slim lozenge while the *mascle* is a *voided lozenge* and the *rustre* (rarely found) is a lozenge with a round hole. These forms are seldom found as a single charge but are usually *conjoined* in the direction of an ordinary. Where a bendlet sinister and a bendlet interlace with a mascle a *fret* is formed.

CROSSES

voided

quarter
pierced

fimbriated

parted and
fretty

Latin

Calvary

patriarchal

fylfot

formy or
paty

crosslet

formy
fitchy

fourché

flory

moline

patonce

botonny

potent

Tau or
St Anthony

Maltese

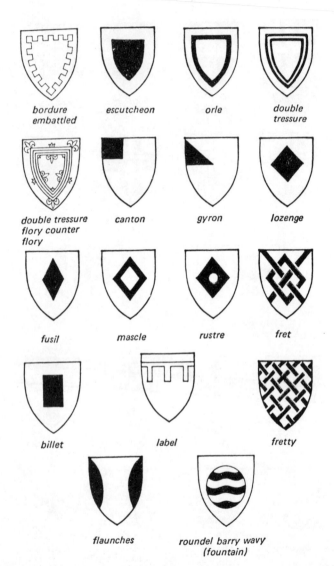

bordure
embattled

escutcheon

orle

double
tressure

double tressure
flory counter
flory

canton

gyron

lozenge

fusil

mascle

rustre

fret

billet

label

fretty

flaunches

roundel barry wavy
(fountain)

24

The curved *flaunches* or *flasques* are always borne in pairs and are rarely drawn with ornamental lines. *Roundels* have been given special names according to their tincture, or may be of fur or may scatter the field or spot an animal. A roundel or is a *bezant* and forms a *bezanty* field, similarly a roundel argent is a *plate*, thus *platy*, and a roundel azure is a *hurt*, thus *hurty*.

Barry wavy argent and azure is an heraldic fountain or *syke* (well). An *annulet* is a voided roundel, a plain ring.

The *label* as a charge is usually drawn from one side of the shield to the other, usually in chief and usually with three or five *points* or bands.

A few of the oldest shields of arms consist of a single tincture, such as the ermine shield of Brittany and the thirteenth-century vair shield of Hugh de Ferrers; more display party fields and fields charged simply with the ordinaries and subordinaries. But representational charges were used from the beginning and some had readily recognised pre-heraldic associations, such as the royal lion and imperial eagle. Because of the continuing need to individualise arms almost any object, animate or inanimate, may be used as an heraldic device.

OBJECT CHARGES

Animals

Animals have figured in heraldry from early days, either whole or in parts, with the lion taking the foremost place. They added variety for the heralds and were popular with armigers both for their implied qualities and the scope for canting arms, where the name of the charge contained the name of the armiger.

Where the charge consists of a part only it is most often the head, which is precisely described to indicate how it is to be depicted. Usually the head is in profile, with or without a neck. *Couped* indicates a head cut off straight at the neck; *couped close* means cut off leaving no neck. *Erased*, meaning torn off, indicates a jagged edge at the neck. A *caboshed* head is full face with no neck, but a lion's face is blazoned *face*. This charge and the leopard's face is sometimes found with a fleur-de-lis through the mouth and is then *jessant-de-lis*. A lion may also be crowned. A fox's head is a *mask* and a horse's head may be a *nag's head*.

Where applicable the beast is said to be *langued* (of the tongue if other than gules) and *armed* (of horns and tusks), and the colour is indicated. The bristles on a boar's head may be a different colour — *crined* or *bristled* of the tincture — and he may be *muzzled* (as may a bear). A stag's antlers are *attires* and it is *attired*. Hounds are usually the *talbot* or the *greyhound* and their necks may be *collared*. A bull with a ring through its nose is *ringed*.

When the top half of the animal is the charge it is a *demibeast* and is depicted *rampant* (erect), though this is not blazoned. Most frequently found are the lion (with the tuft of the tail as well), bear, wolf and bull, and mainly as a crest. The legs and paws of lions and bears and the leg of the bull occur occasionally but not nearly so frequently as stag's attires and horseshoes.

Where the whole animal is depicted descriptions of the head may apply and in addition it is stated whether it is armed (of claws unless gules) or *unguled* or hoofed. A greyhound may be collared and *leashed*, a horse *bridled* or, if fully equipped for riding, *furnished* or *caparisoned*. A bear may be *muzzled, collared and chained;* an elephant may carry a castle.

The most familiar terms are those applied to the attitude and posture of the animal. The pre-eminent heraldic beast is the lion, borne on the shields of the great and powerful. Originally it was depicted *rampant* (erect), in profile, standing on one paw. Then changing shapes of shield, artistic necessity and the popularity of the charge prompted major and minor variations — there are at least forty ways of depicting the lion. When posture is described one word may suffice, for example rampant, which means erect, in profile, standing on one hind paw, tail erect. Should the lion be required to look towards the observer, however, the head position must be described, for example lion rampant *guardant*. Finally, the position of the tail is again implied in rampant but should there be a variation, for example a double tail, the blazon would be rampant guardant *double queued*.

All the beasts share this terminology more or less. There are some special terms, some animals are rarely depicted in more than one posture and no beast equals the versatility of the lion, whose principal postures follow, with notes on terms describing other beasts.

The front of the lion is to the dexter, the rear to the sinister, unless blazoned otherwise.

Rampant: erect, in profile, one hind paw on the ground, the other three raised, tail erect. A *goat* may be blazoned *climant:* a griffin, *ségreant.*

Salient: springing — both hind paws on the ground, both fore paws raised, tail erect. A horse is *forcene.*

Passant: walking — three paws on the ground, dexter fore paw raised, looking forward, tail curved over the back. A horse

Clockwise from top: lion rampant, tail nowed; lion sejant guardant erect; lion rampant queue fourché; lions rampant combatant; lion rampant double queued; demi-lion rampant. Centre: lion's head couped.

may be *trotting* or, at full stretch, *courant*; a deer *trippant* or, at full stretch, *courant*, *at speed* or *in full chase*; a dog *trippant* or, chasing another animal, *in full chase* or *in full course*; the rabbit or *coney courant*.

Statant: standing — as passant but with all four paws on the ground.

Sejant: seated — with fore paws on the ground, looking forward, tail passing between the legs and then erect. Other seated animals are depicted with their tails in the usual

27

Stag's head erased. Buck's head couped. Stag courant.

Heraldic antelope rampant: Heraldic tiger passant. Bengal tiger passant.

position. The *squirrel* is always sejant, usually cracking a nut.

Sejant rampant or *erect:* as sejant but with fore paws raised.

Affronty: showing the full front — always sejant for a lion.

Couchant: crouching — legs and belly on the ground, looking forward, tail passing between the legs and then erect. A deer with legs bent under is *lodged.*

Dormant: as couchant, but with head lowered and tail on the ground.

Head positions
Guardant: head towards the observer. A deer is *at gaze.*

Reguardant: having head turned back to look over the shoulder.

Tail descriptions
These apply only to lions except for *coward.*

Extended: straight out behind.

Coward: between the legs. The *lynx* is nearly always blazoned coward.

Nowed: in a knot.

Queue fourché or *double queued:* double-tailed.

28

The heraldic lion is a majestic figure in most positions, familiarly stylised up to modern times. The lions of England were conventionally blazoned as *leopards* from the French practice of describing a walking lion as a leopard to distinguish it from a lion which was always rampant. More than four lions may still be called *lioncels* (little lions), whatever their size, but this is now rare. Lions rampant back to back are *addorsed*; rampant face to face they are *combatant* or *counter rampant*. There are some double-headed, two- or three-bodied lions, winged lions and dismembered lions.

There are a few heraldic distinctions in the deer family. While the bodies may be very similar, the *stag* or *hart* has a full head of antlers, the *buck* has broad flat antlers and the *hind* has none at all. The *springbok, reindeer, elk* and *antelope* are represented naturally. The *heraldic antelope* is quite different, having a fierce pointed head with protruding tongue, serrated horns and a long tufted tail.

The *heraldic tiger* is a curious creature which early artists had heard of but probably never seen! It has a wolflike head,

Lynx coward. Leopard's head jessant-de-lis. Leopard passant guardant. Fox's mask.

Boar's head couped. Bear muzzled, collared and chained. Wolf salient. Boar statant.

with pointed ears and tusks, adorned with a lion's mane, on a lion's body. After India was acquired the *Bengal tiger* entered British heraldry and is depicted as in nature. Leopards as found in nature do not appear often in English heraldry; the *ounce* is identical. The *cat* is usually called *wild cat* or *cat-a-mountain;* it is usually tabby and appears more in Irish and Scottish heraldry. Panthers are dealt with in the next section.

The *wolf* is found quite often, not always very wolflike in early heraldry and common as a head only, especially in Scottish heraldry. The *fox* is very similar but its mask is quite distinctive; the *lynx* is almost identical.

Bears are usually muzzled and in the famous arms of Warwick a bear supports a ragged staff. The *boar* may be termed *sanglier*, a wild boar, and occasionally a boar's head will be blazoned 'erect' and is shown with the mouth upwards.

The *horse* is depicted naturally. There is a *seahorse* with a fish tail and webbed forefeet, perhaps with a fin instead of a mane on the neck, and the *pegasus* or winged horse is often a supporter or crest.

Besides the traditional talbot and greyhound, *mastiffs, fox-hounds,* and even a *sleuth hound* have been shown and in the twentieth century spaniels, yellow labradors, old English sheepdogs and others have been introduced.

Oxen, cows and *calves* seem to be most frequent in canting arms, as is the *bull,* which is also found, winged, as a supporter of the arms of the Butchers' Company. The *ram* is represented with horns and the *sheep* without, most often passant and statant. The skin of a girdled ram (with a strap around its middle) is a *fleece.* A *lamb* is often found with a halo and a cross as the *Holy Lamb* or *Paschal lamb.* Goats and goats' heads appear frequently.

The *elephant and castle* appears in some arms as do *tusks,* and *elephant's heads* are found more often than the entire animal. The curious curved horns with open ends, which are derived from the Viking-type horns on helmets, are described quite wrongly in English heraldry as *elephant's trunks.*

Of the smaller animals, squirrels, rabbits and badgers are found more often than hares, otters, stoats and weasels. The hedgehog figures as the *hurcheon, urchin, herrison* and *herizon.* These and other animals are usually brought in for canting arms.

Monsters

The heraldic antelope and tiger mentioned above fall into the category of heraldic monsters, which derived from the efforts of early artists either to depict creatures they had not

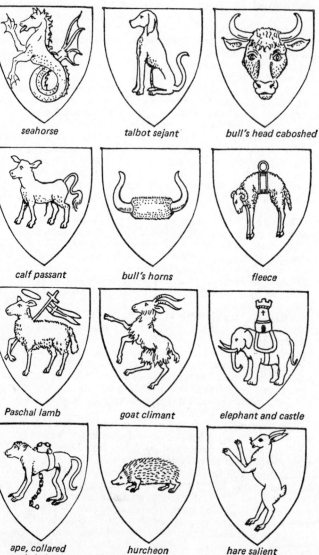

seahorse

talbot sejant

bull's head caboshed

calf passant

bull's horns

fleece

Paschal lamb

goat climant

elephant and castle

ape, collared
and chained

hurcheon

hare salient

31

seen and alleged hybrids of known animals or to interpret descriptions of classical and medieval monsters. The objective was decorative distinction between arms, not realism; conventions in representation were recognised and established very early.

Though origins are largely conjectural some explanations recommend themselves. The *cameleopard* is a giraffe, which seems a very likely rationalisation into a hybrid of two animals which were known. The *dragon* is, perhaps, at heart a crocodile. Akin to the dragon is the *griffin* or *gryphon*, which has the body, hind legs and tail of a lion with the head, ears, wings and foreclaws of an eagle. The *opinicus* substitutes the tail of a bear. A *wyvern* has the head and forefeet of a dragon attached to a scaly curved tail. A wyvern with a cock's head, comb and wattles is a *cockatrice*. English heraldry features a *male griffin*, which is not winged but has spikes on the body. The hybrid lion and eagle was really credited so it is scarcely surprising that the unicorn was universally believed in until the seventeenth century.

A *unicorn* has an antelope's body, a horse's head, a long twisted horn and a beard, a lion's tail, stag's legs and cloven hoofs. Pliny told of horned horses; crusaders saw antelopes which might have appeared single-horned in profile, and unicorn's horn was marketed in Europe. Ground horn was included in medieval medical prescriptions, where its use was based on the theory that the noble qualities of the animal resided in it.

While the tailed *merman* or *triton* is not often found in English heraldry, the *mermaid* with glass and comb is quite frequently depicted. A *melusine* is a two-tailed mermaid, more common in Germany than Britain, as is the *centaur*, half man, half horse, frequently found *sagitarrius*, carrying a bow and arrow. The *sphinx* has the body of a lion with the head, face and breasts of a woman. More commonly found in Germany is the *harpy*, the head and upper body of a woman with the wings and lower body of a vulture.

Greek mythology provided the *phoenix*, often shown as a demi-eagle, issuing from flames of fire, and the winged horse, *pegasus*. Another fiery creature is the lizard-like *salamander* amid flames, alternatively depicted as a fire-breathing dog with a lion's tail. The heraldic *panther* breathes fire from its mouth and ears and is often spattered with roundels. This was not always so but, particularly in continental heraldry, the legend of the gaily spotted panther whose sweet breath repelled dragons influenced its metamorphosis to fabulous beast.

The *enfield* is an extraordinary hybrid with a fox's head on a wolf's body and the forelegs and talons of an eagle. More

dragon

griffin

male griffin

opinicus

wyvern

cockatrice

unicorn

melusine

centaur

sphinx

harpy

phoenix

3   33

obvious is the *sea-lion* with a lion's body ending in a fish's tail: most animals and monsters with the exception of dogs and wolves can be made into sea-creatures by substituting a tail for the hind legs and adding the odd fin.

| salamander | heraldic panther | enfield |

Birds

The attitudes of birds in heraldry have their descriptions:

Closed or *trussed:* standing with wings folded.

Perched: perched on an object.

Rising or *rousant:* when about to fly and, then, according to wing position:

   a. *Displayed:* affronty with head turned, wings and legs spread, tips up.

   b. *Displayed, wings inverted:* as displayed with tips down.

   c. *Wings elevated and displayed:* one wing spread on each side, tips upwards.

   d. *Wings displayed and inverted:* wings spread, tips downwards.

   e. *Wings elevated and addorsed:* wings spread back to back, tips up.

   f. *Wings addorsed and inverted:* wings spread back to back, tips down.

Soaring: flying upwards.

Volant: flying horizontally.

The eagle is king of the birds, the symbol of power. The device of the Romans and Charlemagne, it carried imperial connotations until the twentieth century. In heraldry the two-headed eagle was the emblem of the Holy Roman Empire and hence of Austria and Germany and also of Russia. Napoleon had a single-headed eagle as did the modern German Empire. Conventionally represented from early days it is also found holding the shield or represented by a part, a head or wing for example. The *osprey* is always a white eagle.

Falcons are like eagles but with smooth heads and necks.

When bells are attached by thongs to the legs they are *belled* and *jessed* and they may be depicted *hooded*. The heraldic *dove* or *columb* has a tuft at the back of the head and often bears an olive branch in its beak. The heraldic swallow is called a *martlet* and is depicted without feet; the ordinary

Eagle rising, wings elevated and addorsed. Double-headed eagle displayed. Falcon displayed, wings inverted, belled and jessed.

Eagle's wing. Eagle's head couped. Dove rising. Martlet volant.

Pelican in her piety. Peacock in its pride. Swan rousant.

Cornish chough. Crane in its vigilance. Stork. Moorcock.

swallow retains his feet. Ravens, crows and rooks are indistinguishable and are usually simply termed *corbie*. Similar is the popular *Cornish chough*, distinguished by red legs and red beak.

The *swan* is a popular charge and peacocks shown affronty are blazoned *a peacock in its pride*. The *crane* is usually depicted *in its vigilance*, with a stone in its claw (if the bird falls asleep and drops the stone it will wake up). The *stork* looks similar but sometimes has a snake in its beak and must be distinguished from the *heron*, which may be holding an eel. However, the heron is usually tufted. The *ostrich* usually has a metal horseshoe or other indigestible object in its beak.

The domestic *cock* is sometimes termed *dunghill cock* to distinguish it from the *game cock*, which has a cut comb and exaggerated spurs, and the *moorcock*, which is the farmyard cock with a gamebird's tail.

The heraldic *pelican*, often an ecclesiastical charge, is usually standing on a nest, pecking at her breast — *vulning* herself. Usually blazoned *a pelican in its piety*, it signifies the sacrifice of Christ or maternal devotion.

Where beaks and legs are of a different tincture they are said to be *beaked and legged* (or *membered*) of the tincture. Birds of prey may be said to be *armed* of a tincture. The cock is *armed* or *spurred* and *combed* (crested) and *jelopped* (referring to the wattles).

Fish

The type of fish is not always blazoned but the position is. *Naiant* means swimming (fesswise); if *urinant* or *uriant* the fish is diving (in pale) with head in base; when *hauriant* it is rising (palewise), the head upwards.

Most fish are depicted according to nature, but the *dolphin* has a broad indented fin along a body *embowed*, bent in a curve. Salmon appear more frequently in British armoury than whales for example, and much *punning* use is made of *roach*, *pike (lucy)* and others.

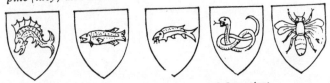

Dolphin embowed. Pike. Barbel. Serpent nowed. Bee volant.

Reptiles

British serpents are usually quite naturalistic, *nowed* (knotted), *erect* or *glissant* (gliding), but in other countries they are much more menacing. Lizards, scorpions, newts and even horseleeches can be found, one or two snails, some toads, but apparently no frogs.

Insects

The *bee* is the most popular insect, depicted as seen from above with extended wings — *volant*. It became important in French armoury when Napoleon adopted it as a badge. The *grasshoppers* of the Gresham family are now famous as the golden grasshoppers of the City of London. Ants, butterflies, crickets, gadflies and even fleas and flies have all been used as charges.

Flora

A tree is an oak tree unless named otherwise (which it often is for canting purposes). Growing without roots showing on a green mound it is *issuant from a mount vert*. With roots it is *eradicated.* A clump of trees is a *hurst*. Shades of empire may be detected in coffee, coconut and palm trees, sometimes *fructed* of their fruit (an oak is *acorned*).

Trunks and *stocks* of trees occur and so do *branches* (usually of laurel, palm, holly or oak) and *slips* — leaves and sprigs on the stem. *Leaves,* particularly of distinctive shape, appear. The heraldic *trefoil*, probably a shamrock, *quatrefoil* and *cinquefoil* are old devices.

The English heraldic *rose* is the hedgerow dog rose with five displayed petals; the *Tudor rose* shows a double row. A rose may be any colour so the tincture must be blazoned but if it is *barbed and seeded proper* the sepals will be green and the seeded centre gold and if *slipped and leaved proper* it will have green stem and leaves.

Fleurs-de-lis are found everywhere, though most significantly as the emblem of the French monarchs. Though first borne heraldically by Louis VII of France in the twelfth century (hence, perhaps, 'fleurs de Louis') and immediately stereotyped in representation, their emblematic existence is much older. The true *lily* is a quite distinct charge, more like the flower in nature.

The *thistle*, slipped and leaved proper, appeared quite late as a badge of the Scottish sovereign. When the blazon *pineapple* occurs it means fircone except in a few instances. *Pomegranates*, *grapes* and *cloves* appear individually, as well as more common fruit. *Ears* of grain and *clusters* of wheat are found

Oak tree eradicated. Trefoil and quatrefoil. Cotton tree fructed proper.

Rose slipped and leaved. Garden lily. Thistle. Sprig of lime slipped and leaved. Garb.

Fleurs-de-lis

but sheafs or *garbs* are more common. Reeds, bulrushes, and even grass appear.

Human figure

As a charge on a shield the human figure is infrequent, parts of the body less so. Sacred characters are found in some ecclesiastical and civic arms, for example our Lord seated upon a throne of gold (See of Chichester), the Virgin and Child (Royal Burgh of Banff), St Peter and St Paul (Borough of Wisbech). Divine and human figures are found as supporters and as crests.

The human figure is a relatively unadaptable charge, requiring detail or characterisation to be interesting. Conventional symbols like *Justice*, blindfolded and with sword and scales, depict well, as does a *man in armour*. Naked *savages*, wreathed at head and loins, appear, but more often the head only is used and there are recognised types, such as *blackamoor's, Saracen's* and *Saxon's*, and they appear affronty or in profile, couped or erased.

The arm is found quite often and has its own terminology. A *cubit* arm is cut off at the elbow; an *arm embowed* is the whole arm bent at the elbow with clenched fist pointing upwards. It may be *proper* (naked), *vambraced* (in armour), *habited* or *vested* and *cuffed* (clothed). Its position should be stated, for example fesswise, and whether dexter or sinister.

A *hand* may be appaumy (open, showing the palm) or *closed*. *Legs* may be couped or erased at thigh or knee. *Bones, skulls* and *hearts* are found.

Inanimate objects

Anything may be a charge but, as there are among the older devices some stylised representations which are not immediately recognisable and others with traditional blazons, several are shown.

Upper left: justice. Lower left: three dexter arms vambraced and embowed. Centre: arms of Marylebone. Upper right: Saracen's head. Lower right: dexter hand in benediction.

anchor

arrow

pheon

broad arrow

battleaxe

Danish axe

battering ram

beacon

church bell

hawk bell

billhook

cannon

castle

tower

chess rook

dividers

ecclesiastical
hat

fleam

fasces

firebomb

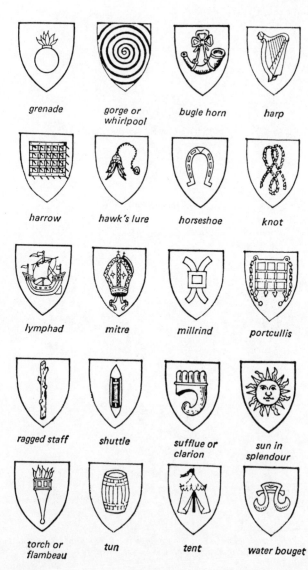

grenade

gorge or whirlpool

bugle horn

harp

harrow

hawk's lure

horseshoe

knot

lymphad

mitre

millrind

portcullis

ragged staff

shuttle

sufflue or clarion

sun in splendour

torch or flambeau

tun

tent

water bouget

41

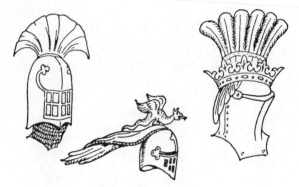

Fan-shaped crest. Animate crest. Panache.

Top left: striking but impossible rainbow crest. Top right: correct side-ways crest and helm. Centre: sideways crest, affronty helm.

4. The completed picture

A shield alone would fulfil the principal purpose of heraldry to show the man in his family as distinct from all others. But, compared with the glory of a full achievement, the shield is like a synopsis of a full account which tells more about the family and where the armiger stands among his contemporaries.

The type of helm ensigning the shield, its position and display rising from a coronet, and the presence or absence of supporters indicate the armiger's rank; the crest may reflect his own interests and achievements or those of his ancestors; ancient pride and ambition and dedication to duty are preserved in many mottoes; service to queen and country may be shown in the display of the insignia of an order of chivalry or military decorations.

Gratifying as a full achievement is to the armiger, the scope offered as the concept developed must have gladdened the hearts of heraldic artists, who seized the opportunity to compose fine displays of artistic unity which were vigorous, imaginative and individual, governed by the same heraldic rules but applied more flexibly.

Tilting helm.

The helm and crest

The idea of including a helm and its crest in the representational display of arms presumably arose from the observation that, as crests were all different and some had hereditary or other special significance or were derived from associated devices, they were as distinctive in their way as shields.

The helm on which the crest has usually been displayed was the pot helm or great helm. Because it was so big and cumbersome, it was eventually superseded in battle by lighter forms of protection for the head and neck and its use was restricted to the tournament, hence its place in heraldry. The three main types — the enclosed tilting helm with only a narrow slit to peer through, the vizored helm for use in hand-to-hand combat, and the barred or latticed helm for the increased hazards of the melée — have been depicted (with a few diversionary flights of fancy in the post-tournament era)

43

down to the present day. They are shown affronty or sideways according to rank, applying the following rules:

For the sovereign and princes of the blood: a barred helm of gold, affronty.

For a peer: a five-barred helm of silver, decorated with gold, sideways.

For a baronet or knight: a vizored helm of steel, vizor raised, decorated with silver, affronty.

For an esquire, gentleman or corporate body: a closed or closed vizored helm of steel, sideways.

All open helms may be lined.

Closed helm. Helm with vizor raised, affronty. Five-barred helm, sideways.

The crest

The crest is an important part of the achievement (the word is derived from Latin *crista*, a cock's comb); until crests were introduced helms were not depicted. The 'comb' ran from the forehead over the crown (something like the ridge on a fireman's helmet) and was originally a reinforcement to lessen the impact of a blow. It tended to become more or less fan-shaped, taller or broader, scalloped or plain, according to taste.

In the twelfth and thirteenth centuries this projection was probably distinctively painted, like the body armour, with colours and devices associated with the wearer, and it was a natural progression to shape the fan to produce a representational outline. At the same time the *panache*, a cluster of feathers, appeared as a form of crest; some were very impressive, with three or four tiers rising from the helm.

It is clear that no one could undertake serious fighting in war with more than a token crest. Indeed the great helm was only used in tournaments from the fifteenth century and the development of the modelled crest belongs to the tournaments of the Plantagenets. It would be possible to endure the added weight and height of an elaborate crest for a course or two or in a ceremonial parade.

Every effort was made to render the crest as light as pos-

44

sible: boiled leather or cloth was moulded over a wooden or wire framework and ballast was provided by tow, sawdust or even sponge. Animate crests were always preferred and as a result many crests ceased to relate to the arms.

Under the code of chivalry not every man entitled to bear arms was entitled to compete in the tournament and it appears that the use of a crest in an achievement was at first restricted to those whose rank qualified them to take part. It was early on in the Tudor period that crests began to be granted regularly as additions to existing arms which had not qualified earlier. Subsequently few grants were made without a crest and since the eighteenth century a personal achievement has included a crest.

With the disappearance of the tournament and of the old forms of armour in war, the crest no longer needed to be capable of physical existence on top of a helm and in England this led eventually to the creation of crests of such elaboration and improbability that they could never have adorned a helm (which suffered similar unrealistic treatment). The problem of suitability was exacerbated by the English rules for the position of the helm, facing forward or sideways according to rank, and compounded by the requirement that crests must be differentiated. In Scotland a crest need not be unique so crests are usually simpler and more suitable and may be changed when the arms are matriculated.

In Germany, where crests are very important and linked to territorial holdings, a single coat may be surmounted by several crests and helms — as many as thirteen. In England five appears to be the largest number and is very unusual — generally the use of more than one can only be granted by Royal Licence. Where there are two crests they may face one another or face dexter, the dexter one being principal. If there are three, the principal one may be on a helm, the other two flanking and unattached. Marks of cadency are used on royal crests but are now unusual on others.

Wreath, chapeau, crest-coronet and crowns

The point at which the crest was attached to the helm by rivets or laces seems to have been disguised in various ways, for example by twisting around it a plain band of cloth or a lady's 'favour', and from this developed the *wreath* or *torse* of heraldry. It is shown now as a twisted ribbon of two or more tinctures.

Originally the colours of the torse do not appear to have related to the arms but from the end of the sixteenth century the wreath' has been *of the colours* of the principal metal and tincture 'of the arms, the metal appearing first, of six

45

twists. Recently different tinctures have been allowed and sometimes more than two.

The *chapeau* or cap of maintenance appears to derive from a combination of the protective *capelot* once used on the helm before mantling appeared and the cap of dignity originally reserved to royalty and peers. It is of red velvet with an ermine turn-up ending in two points. As a basis for the crest it did descend the social scale but is now granted rarely and only to peers and, in Scotland, to feudal barons.

It would save confusion if a crest coronet, which may be blazoned *ducal coronet*, were called something else. It originated as a metal alternative to or embellishment of the torse or wreath and took several foliated and floral forms — officially now a circlet of fleurs-de-lis. It appears sometimes on a wreath but it is seldom granted now.

There are some special forms of coronet, used as a basis for a crest or to ensign the arms or badges, usually with specific applications. The *mural crown* is used in civic heraldry, particularly in Scotland, and in the arms of distinguished soldiers, as it is masoned and embattled. It is often now used in place of a crest. Similarly a *naval crown* with sterns and sails of ships has been displayed by notable sailors and both branches of the navy. Distinguished service in the East has warranted the inclusion of the *eastern crown* of eight broad points; in aviation, of the *astral crown* of four winged stars. There are *vallary*, *palisado* and *ancient* crowns as well.

First row: crest on cap of maintenance; mural crown.
Second row: palisado crown; astral crown; naval crown.

46

Mantling

It is supposed that the ornamental drapery flowing from the helm originated from the need to insulate the metal helm from the heat of the sun with a small mantle, which predictably was made into a handsome adjunct to the outfit. It was usually of the principal colour of the arms *doubled* (lined) with another colour and had scalloped edges. It could be patterned or spattered with badges. Later red and silver mantling was nearly always used but nowadays it may be of any colour and more than two, save only that gold lined with ermine is reserved for the Crown and royal princes and ermine lining for peers.

Crowns and coronets of rank

The crowns and coronets which indicate rank in English heraldry are still used ceremonially and are not purely pictorial as are most of the other elements in the achievement.

The heraldic royal crown is borne on the royal helm, as is the coronet of the heir apparent. The circlet of four crosses formy alternating with four fleurs-de-lis comes from the crown of Henry VI; today it is depicted adorned with emeralds, rubies and sapphires. Springing from the circlet are four quarter arches, three showing, the two at the side each carrying nine pearls, the front arch carrying five. For the crown of Charles II the arches were depressed at the centre, which bears the mound surmounted by a cross (from the crown of Henry V). The cap inside is crimson with an ermine lining, which appears, turned up, at the base of the circlet. The coronet of the heir apparent differs in having only one round arch.

Coronets are shown resting on the shield with the helm rising above. When depicted in their entirety they each have a crimson cap bearing a central gold tassel but no arches over and are differentiated by the disposition around the circlet of crosses (in the case of royalty), fleurs-de-lis, strawberry leaves and pearls (actually silver balls). When represented in arms the cap is not necessarily shown. The circlet is chased as jewelled except for that of a baron.

Sons, daughters, brothers and sisters of the Sovereign display a circlet of alternating four crosses paly and four fleurs-de-lis (showing three crosses and two fleurs-de-lis). Children of the heir apparent replace the two side crosses with strawberry leaves. Children of the sovereign's brothers and younger sons replace the fleurs-de-lis with strawberry leaves. Children of the sovereign's daughters alternate four fleurs-de-lis and four strawberry leaves.

baron

viscount

earl

marquess

duke

royal crown

Coronets assigned to the peerage are easier to recognise. A duke shows five of his eight strawberry leaves rising from the circlet. A marquess substitutes four pearls and four fleurs-de-lis alternately. An earl has eight strawberry leaves interspersed with eight smaller pearls on spikes, of which five pearls and four fleurs-de-lis are shown. Sixteen pearls set touching each other top the circlet of a viscount, and nine of them are shown. A baron has eight large pearls, four showing.

At the end of the eighteenth century the arms of a peer were frequently shown on a *robe of estate* in the display on carriage panels. This is a parliamentary robe, depicted as a scarlet cloth lined with taffeta, degrees of rank being distinguished by the guards or bands of fur shown. For example, a duke has four guards of ermine, each edged with gold lace tied up to the left shoulder. Continental heraldry made much more use of the robe of estate, particularly where, as in France and Italy, helmets and crests were less popular. Similar is the pavilion, unknown in British heraldry, a tent-shaped robe usually in purple or red and lined with ermine, surmounted by a crown and used by royalty and high aristocracy.

48

Supporters

In English heraldry supporters are usually found in pairs, one on either side of the shield. They do not appear in achievements until the fourteenth century and seem to have been a by-product of the important heraldic business of designing seals. Here artists had greater flexibility and embellished the central theme of the arms by filling the flanking spaces with associated devices, such as badges. Until the late fourteenth century they were decorative and occasional and until the middle of the sixteenth century they were not properly controlled. Animals and birds, human and imaginary figures were popular from the beginning and usually had some prior association with the armiger.

Ape supporters in the arms of the Duke of Leinster.

Only the nobility had a variety of such devices to draw upon so when true supporters came regularly into the system in the mid fifteenth century they tended to appear in only the more illustrious achievements and never became usual in grants. Today supporters are restricted to peers, knights first class of the orders of chivalry and of the Garter, Thistle and St Patrick, district and parish councils (if of town status) and some corporations. Only hereditary peers transmit supporters by inheritance.

The English predilection for differencing created similar, though fewer, artistic and practical problems with supporters as it did with crests. Scottish heraldry requires no difference.

As supporters are usually animate they are depicted standing or rampant. Of human beings savages and men in armour are most common and angels appear quite often. Lions, sometimes winged, griffins and other fabulous beasts make equally impressive flanking figures. Eagles are used and Glasgow has two salmon, but there is some feeling that the figures used should appear to be capable of a supportive role. In the few instances where inanimate objects are found their lack of capacity is acknowledged and the shield is said to be *cotised*, that is, has one on each side. Lighted torches, pillars of Hercules, tent poles and trees are examples.

Footing for the supporters is supplied by the compartment. Originally a representation of solid ground was depicted, but flimsy scrolls and platforms had periods of popularity. When a grassy mound was the norm the compartment was not usually described in the blazon and there was plenty of scope for the artist. Today the compartment is blazoned.

Orders of knighthood

By implication a knight was a military man who held his rank by virtue of the services he was expected to perform for his feudal superior and, exclusively since Henry III, for the king. It was possible to commute his obligations by the payment of a fine, for some knights were unfitted, indisposed or unable to perform useful service.

Within the ranks of knighthood there were special groups for which a knight might be selected or which he might, if qualified, join. These were the orders of knighthood, which had their distinctive insignia; for example, the Knights of St John of Jerusalem, 1092, and the Knights of the Temple, or Templars, 1140, were orders originating in the Crusades. Orders of chivalry such as the Garter also had their own insignia.

In the fifteenth century Garter Knights sometimes encircled their shields with the Garter in their achievements. From the sixteenth century it was generally included. These days the shield is encircled by the Garter, bearing in gold letters the motto *Honi soit qui mal y pense*. The gold collar of garters interspersed with knots may be placed outside the Garter, from which hangs the badge of St George on horseback slaying the dragon.

As other orders were formed their members were allowed to dispose the insignia similarly. For example, a knight of the Most Noble Order of the Thistle surrounds his shield with the green circlet edged in green bearing in gold letters the motto *Nemo me impune lacessit*. The collar is gold with alternate sprigs of thistle and rue. The badge of St Andrew, bearing his white saltire, on an eight-pointed star-shaped green background hangs from the collar.

Members below the rank of Commander or Companion

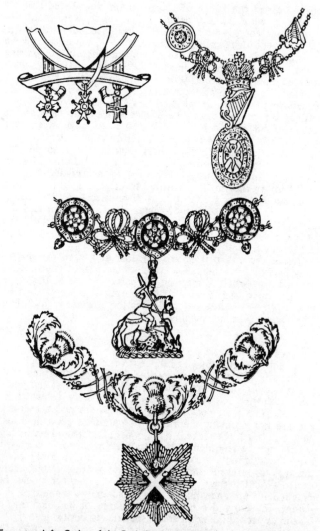

From top left: Order of the Bath flanked by OBE and MC; collar and badge of the Order of St Patrick; collar and badge of the Order of the Garter; collar and badge of the Order of St Andrew.

may suspend the badge of the order on the ribbon. Knights Bachelor, who did not belong to an order, were granted a badge by George V and since 1973 have been allowed to suspend it beneath their arms. Since Charles I, Baronets of Nova Scotia (instituted in 1625 in connection with colonising there), have had a badge and in 1929 all other Baronets were granted one. This, too, may be shown beneath the arms.

Medals and decorations awarded by the Crown (and foreign orders with royal permission) may be displayed. Certain offices under the crown have special insignia, such as the collar of SS of the Lord Chief Justice of England and the gold batons tipped with black in saltire behind the shield of the Earl Marshal and Hereditary Marshal of England, the Duke of Norfolk. Members of the order of St John of Jerusalem may display the insignia according to their grade.

Where an individual is entitled to display insignia of more than one order or office it is usual to select only the principal order. Otherwise the principal circlet is shown and the principal collar with the lesser collar outside. Similarly the badge of the senior order is centred below, with orders to dexter and sinister in order of seniority.

As orders and offices are personal and, save for specifically hereditary ranks such as baronetcies, not transmitted, insignia are displayed only on the paternal arms of the member if a man and on the married arms of a woman placed next to her husband's paternal arms to show she is the holder (see chapter 5 on marshalling).

Mottoes

Where a motto appears in a coat of arms most people are sufficiently intrigued to study it though they know nothing about heraldry and have little Latin. It is regarded as a significant indication of the attitude of the family to which it belongs. Yet in English heraldry mottoes are not hereditary and are not normally mentioned in a grant of personal arms, and no authority is needed to use one; in impersonal grants the motto may be recorded in the blazon. No control is exercised over the wording — although heralds would probably exert pressure to prevent the appearance of a totally unsuitable motto — and it may be placed above or below the shield. In practice its presence may be recorded in the margin of the patent. In Scotland a motto is hereditary, is included in the blazon as part of the grant and is specifically positioned.

Although mottoes appear in the fourteenth and fifteenth centuries they do not occur with any regularity before the eighteenth. Some may have origins as war cries or slogans

(*Dieu et mon droit* — Richard I at Gisons in 1198) but a more likely origin is as part of the badge. Quite a few are ancient or at least refer to historic or imaginary moments of glory. Many use the words, in Latin, French, English or in translation, as a reference to the arms (*canting*) or a pun on the name. Others are rebus mottoes, in which the name appears amongst the words of the motto. Clever ones combine historical with canting or rebus elements.

Ranulf de Mesnilwaren was one of the first invading Normans to leap ashore at Pevensey, allegedly crying '*Devant si je puis*' ('Foremost if I can') and the Mainwaring family subsequently adopted his words as their motto. The Fitzgerald family recall a bizarre family incident in their motto, *Non immemor benefici* ('Grateful for kindness'). The baby Thomas Fitzgerald, orphaned by the battle of Callan and unattended in his cradle, was seized by the family baboon and carried to the top of Tralee Cathedral out of harm's way!

The winnowing fans in the arms of De Setvans were alluded to in the canting motto *Sic dissipatio inimicos Regis mei* — 'Thus (like chaff before the fan) will I scatter my King's enemies'. The Hope name and crest of a rainbow above a broken globe are reflected in *At spes infracta* ('Yet hope is unbroken'). Lesley's *Firma durant* ('Firm things last') refers to buckles in the arms.

Puns are very popular: *Cave deus vidit* ('Beware, God sees') for Cave, *Gare le pied fort* ('Beware the strong foot') — just about Bedford. In translation *Faber mea fortuna* ('Smith of my own fortune') is most apposite for F.E. Smith, first Earl of Birkenhead and a self-made man, *Audax ero* ('I will be bold') is succinct for Boldero and *Fabula sed vera* ('A story but a true one') is graceful for Storey. Almost too subtle is *Ama deum et serva mandata* ('Love God and keep his commandments') for Synnot.

Rebus mottoes are prone to curious spellings: *Per se valens* — Perceval ('Strong in himself'); *Mea dos virtus* — Meadows ('Honour is my dowry'). The name is often well concealed: *Time deum, cole regem* — Coleridge ('Fear God and honour the king'); or revealed in colloquial translation: *Ostendo non ostento* ('I show, I sham not') — Sir Gyles Isham. One of the cleverest is that of Chichester Rural District Council: *Ad huc hic hesterna* ('The things of yesterday are still here').

A neat historical and rebus motto is Fortescue's *Forte scutum salus ducum* ('A strong shield is the safety of leaders'). A Fortescue saved William the Conqueror at Hastings with his shield. An ancestor of the Lockharts named Locard went to the Holy Land having charge of one of the keys to a box containing Robert Bruce's heart. The motto *Corda serata fero*

('I bear a locked heart') is a pun on the altered name as well as a memory of the story.

The Germans enjoy mottoes and have the monopoly of initial or riddle mottoes, such as G W G – *Gottes Willegeschehe* ('God's will be done') – and the celebrated vowel motto. Frederick III defied anyone to interpret what the initials stood for; *Austria est Imperate Orbe Universo* was revealed after his death ('All the earth is subject to Austria'). Forty other versions of vowel motto have been used.

Scottish mottoes conform to some rules. For example, the cadet's motto should answer the chief's. Thus the head of the Clan Campbell has 'Do not forget' and the McIver Campbell's reply is 'I will never forget'. The position of the motto is designated and there may be two.

Finally here are some apposite impersonal mottoes: the National Coal Board – *E tenebris lux* ('Light out of the darkness'); the Metropolitan Water Board – *Et plui super unam civitatem* ('And I caused it to rain on one city'); the National Small-bore Rifle Association – 'Look forward'.

5. Differencing

The simplest way to preserve the distinctive character of individual achievements implicit in the system of heraldry was to expand and modify the range of charges and vary their disposition. From the beginning this method had to be qualified by the hereditary nature of heraldry and the attitudes of a feudal society.

All legitimate children used the family arms and inherited them after their father's death. Thus distinction had to be made between father and son and between son and son. In the next generation branches of the family would need to be distinguished. Thus there arose a system of *differencing for cadency* which indicated both the branch of the senior family and the position in that branch of the armiger.

In early days it was possible to difference arms by modifying the original arms, retaining distinctive features but producing a new composition. This could be done by changing the tinctures of the field or charges, but it was obviously a limited exercise and lost the significance of established distinctive colours. More scope was afforded by the modification of the charges: variations were made in size and number, by the

Modification of tincture.

Modification of charges.

Lutterell arms (left); (centre) differenced by feudal inferiors with charges; (right) differenced with charge and tincture.

insertion of new or related charges, by slightly altering existing charges, all within an accepted framework which preserved the main characteristics of the original arms. The ordinaries and subordinaries, especially the bordure, bend, canton, chevron and label, were useful and could themselves be charged for difference. Crest, mantling, supporters and badges might be modified in this way. Thus the heraldry of a family had a progressive unity.

It is clear that as the coat, duly differenced, was recognised as pertaining to a particular branch of a family it might be preferable to distinguish in the next generation by introducing a single minor charge which carried a definite message, rather than to adapt the coat. This was done quite early and several symbolic charges were used which were standardised in the sixteenth century into *marks of cadency* whereby a specific charge was assigned to sons in order of seniority.

On the paternal arms are borne these charges: by the eldest son a label, until he succeeds his father; by the second son a crescent; by the third a molet; by the fourth a martlet; by the fifth an annulet; by the sixth a fleur-de-lis; by the seventh a rose; by the eighth a cross moline; by the ninth a double quatrefoil.

The mark is usually borne in the chief unless it has to overlap all four quarters of a quartered shield or has been brought in by a particular quarter. Except for eldest sons the differenced coat is permanent, forming the arms of a branch of the family, which may then repeat the process.

It is open to an illegitimate son to prove his paternity and apply for a grant of the arms, which, if granted, will be differenced. Since the eighteenth century a bordure has usually been used, most often wavy but occasionally plain, compony or engrailed. The bendlet sinister was once an alternative but the baton sinister is almost always for royal bastards. A legitimated child of parents not free to marry at the time of his birth must apply as a bastard and will perhaps follow precedent by differencing with a saltire couped. An adopted child may petition to bear his adoptive father's arms, which would be differenced by two chain links, fesswise or palewise. All must obtain a Royal Licence before being granted arms.

The important distinction between differencing in the family and the heraldic principle of individuality is underlined by the cases which came before the Court of Chivalry, the most important being the Scrope-Grosvenor controversy which lasted from 1385 to 1390. The simple coat, azure, a bend or, was claimed by both armigers. Judgement was in favour of Scrope. Richard II deemed it inappropriate to difference for Grosvenor by a bordure as suggested by the courts because that implied blood relationship, so Grosvenor chose another device for his azure shield, a garb or.

For reasons of sentiment or policy a man might have wished to acknowledge his feudal superior in his arms. He might simply incorporate the principal device in his arms, for

Arms differenced for cadency: label, crescent, molet, martlet, annulet, rose.

Marks of cadency: label, crescent, molet, martlet, annulet, fleur-de-lis, rose, cross moline, double quatrefoil.

57

example the wheatsheaves of the Earl of Chester which appear in the arms of Cheshire families. Alternatively, the arms might be differenced by changing the tinctures or by charging ordinaries, or by retaining the disposition of charges and substituting other devices for one group.

Scheme of cadency bordures devised by a former Lyon Clerk Depute, Mr Stodart, applied to heir and second son.

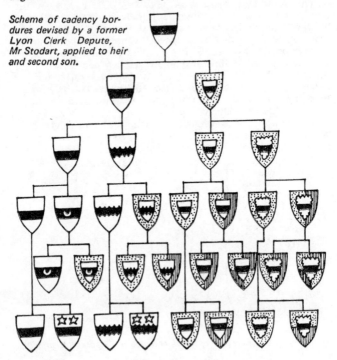

Scotland

The rules of differencing for cadency in Scotland are based on the principle that the coat belongs only to the head of the family at any time. His siblings and his children may only use the arms after they have applied to *matriculate* the arms for personal use. This means that those arms are officially assigned a mark of cadency under a much more controlled and organised system. It is not rigid and the heralds have discretion but certain principles are usually applied.

Differencing for sons is usually effected by the use of bordures of differing tinctures. The children of the eldest son, who has inherited the arms, will probably difference the ordinary with ornamental lines. The children of other sons will similarly ornament the bordure. In the next generation the children of the eldest son may add another charge or ordinary. The children of the other sons may divide the bordure per fess etc, adding another tincture, or vary the ordinary. Each time, the eldest son inherits a coat which passes unchanged to his eldest son on matriculation, so each child except the eldest son has a new, individual coat.

Marshalling

The system of heraldry has so far provided a means of distinguishing a man from all his contemporaries by providing him with a picture he may use. On his seal it identified him more surely than his signature — if he could write. The design indicated quite a lot about him — his family, his rank, his allegiance, perhaps even his name. It was logical, therefore, that he might wish to show additional benefits which came his way, such as the acquisition of further lordships by inheritance or marriage or the holding of an office.

Presented with two or more coats of arms pertaining to one man, the heralds had to decide how best to display them. In early seals several shields were grouped together to form a connected whole — a treatment appropriate to the round shape. It was not so simple to treat shields this way and the early solution here was to take the principal charges and make a new composition on one shield — *compounding* the arms. This method has obvious drawbacks, not least the possible extinction of ancient coats of arms. So the heralds faced the problem of displaying more than one coat on a shield.

Compounded arms: fourteenth-century Duke of Brittany — lions of England, ermine of Brittany; six sets of arms grouped on a seal; dinudiation of England and ships for the Cinque Ports.

At first they tried bisecting each shield and joining the dexter half of one (husband) with the sinister half of the other (wife) — *dimidiation.* Some curious coats were created by this practice and anomalies of identity arose: for example, was it half a chevron to be seen or half a bend? More satisfactory on all counts was the compression of a whole coat into half the shield — *impalement* — and least distorting of all was the division of the shield into quarters, each coat being repeated in the alternate quarter — *quartering.* Marshalling by impalement and quartering soon became the standard methods.

When marshalling takes place

Temporary coats, which will disappear on the death of one of the parties or on divorce or on the ending of a term of office, are distinguished from coats combined permanently, which will be inherited.

The daughter of an armiger bears her father's arms in a simple lozenge and takes them into marriage. If a woman has brothers to transmit the arms to the next generation and has no hereditary rank her arms are combined with her husband's by impalement, hers on the sinister side, his on the dexter, for her lifetime. On her death her arms are removed. On his death she bears the impaled arms on a lozenge. On divorce she reverts to the paternal arms, in a lozenge charged with a mascle.

For the duration of tenure office holders place the official arms in the dexter half of the shield or lozenge. A man and an unmarried or divorced woman put the paternal arms in the sinister half. A married woman should put the marshalled marital arms in the sinister half.

Where a man is entitled to impale his official arms it is with his own arms only, not the combined arms. If he wishes to display both combinations they appear on separate shields side by side, the official arms on the dexter side.

Crests are not transmitted by heiresses and are not displayed except in special cases by royal licence (there were some exceptions in the past). Supporters are hereditary only in the case of peers and peeresses in their own right. When a peeress marries a peer their arms are marshalled on a shield (dexter) and lozenge (without helm or crest), with all the details of the achievement, side by side. On marriage outside the peerage a peeress retains her achievement while her husband charges his own arms, in pretence, with her arms ensigned with her coronet. When grouped together, the shield is to the dexter.

The powerful hereditary element in heraldry is well illustrated in the situation which produces a union of arms which

unmarried woman

impalement

quartering

unmarried man or widower

widow

impaling official arms

union with heiress

widowed heiress

will descend combined. If a woman has no brothers or their sons to continue transmission she is an *heraldic heiress* or, if she has sisters, a *co-heiress*. To prevent the extinction of the arms she takes them into marriage, her husband becomes the temporary representative of the male line and the arms then descend to the children. During the marriage her husband's arms bear in the centre an *escutcheon of pretence* bearing her arms. On her death the escutcheon is removed and representation passes wholly to the children, who bear paternal and maternal arms combined. Should the heiress marry a non-armiger the arms cannot be transmitted unless he subsequently acquires a grant of arms.

Marshalling in practice

The task of the herald is more complicated than appears so far, for the coats to be combined may themselves be the composite results of past alliances. It used to be thought that a family coat should display as much family history of alliance and descent as possible, and this led to complicated genealogical essays in representation. The modern rejection of excess in all directions has largely eliminated shields of multiple subdivisions. Every effort will be made to allude heraldically to illustrious ancestors but preferably by selective quartering or the simple use of devices in a new coat. Nevertheless the rules of marshalling may still be applied and must be understood to interpret older arms. The following examples refer to the diagrams opposite.

The family arms of a woman not an heiress do not pass to her children (a). For the children of an heiress with an unquartered coat the arms are marshalled quarterly to show the paternal coat in the first and third quarters, the maternal coat in the second and fourth, reading from dexter to sinister (b). This coat now represents the two families.

In the next generation a further unquartered coat of an heiress will be marshalled to appear in the third quarter of the shield (c). Future representative coats may be added with additional quarterings as necessary, reading from dexter to sinister top and bottom as before, the father's arms always occupying the first quarter and the last quarter as well if the number is odd (d-f).

An heiress might be representative of more than one family, bringing into marriage a coat already quartered. For her children it is usual in England to break up the quarters and arrange them in order after the paternal coat (g). If it is necessary to retain the maternal coat intact because of conditions of inheritance or its great antiquity or significance it will be quartered entire as a *grand* quarter (h).

Studying the final coat in (g) it seems that alliances have been made by A with heiresses B and C. From (h) it is clear that A married the heiress representing B and C, so it is genealogically accurate. If quarterings are increased the accuracy of the second method is even more marked even though the composition is more complicated. This is the method generally used in Scotland.

It is possible to marshal quarterings selectively providing that it is clear how the quarters shown were brought in. It is not open to the armiger to make a random selection. For example, if he wishes to select one quarter of a representative coat brought in by an heiress it must be the paternal coat which represents the principal alliance; otherwise he must

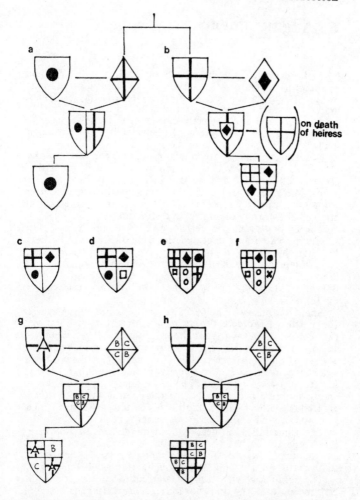

Marshalling in practice.

show the paternal quarter in addition to any other he may
desire.

6. Augmentations

One of the most charming aspects of heraldry is the charging of the arms with an additional device or composition in recognition of outstanding achievement or, in early days, 'of mere grace'. To the arms as they stand is added a charge, crest or quartering which is a distinctly new feature. These are *honourable augmentations* and are marks bestowed by the Sovereign, made by royal warrant.

Grants were made to royal relations and favourites: Richard II granted them to his kinsmen and to Robert de Vere, Earl of Oxford; Edward IV and Henry VIII granted them to their wives. More significant and interesting are those grants given for merit, usually connected with the proper business of an armiger, the bearing of arms with distinction.

The earliest grant was perhaps to Sir William Pelham, who was supposed to have captured the King of France at Poitiers. In 1356 his family arms were quartered with buckles and thongs representing the king's sword belt. Charges from the arms of the Duc de Longueville, captured at the battle of the Spurs in 1513, were put in a canton on the arms of his captor, Sir John Clarke.

Some of those who helped Charles II escape to France after the battle of Worcester were rewarded with augmentations. Colonel Newman, who kept the gate of the city, was granted an *inescutcheon gules, a portcullis imperially crowned or. A canton of England* (three golden lions passant) and a crest of a strawberry roan coupled at the flanks and holding in its feet the Royal Crown were granted to the family of Jane Lane, as whose servant Charles escaped to the coast. A whole coat was granted to Colonel Carlos, another accomplice. (Francis Drake, too, was granted a full coat in augmentation).

The Churchill arms bear two augmentations: *a canton of St George* to Sir Winston Churchill for services to Charles I, and an *inescutcheon of St George* charged with *France Modern* to his son John, Duke of Marlborough, after Blenheim (1704).

The cumulative effect of the augmentations awarded to the Nelson family — the first to Admiral Nelson after the battle of the Nile and the other to the family after Trafalgar — is often cited as a prime example of bad heraldry. The original coat of *or, a cross flory sable surmounted by a bend gules and thereon another engrailed of the field charged with three bombs fired proper* acquired a *chief undy* containing a landscape portraying a palm tree, a disabled ship and a ruined battery. To

Augmentations: (first row) Pelham, buckles; Newman, portcullis imperially crowned; Carlos, entire coat; (second row) Nelson, chief; Howard, shield of Scotland in bend; enlargement showing demi-lion pierced by arrow.

this already lively scene was added a fess *wavy azure*, which covered the horizontal arms of the cross, bearing the word *Trafalgar* in gold letters.

Many heroic deeds resulted in augmentations to arms. Considerably fewer grants were made to salute other forms of achievement. The father of the explorer John Speke, who discovered the source of the Nile, was granted a crest of a crocodile, the word *Nile* on a chief of flowing water and a hippopotamus and a crocodile as supporters. Royal doctors have been favoured on occasions and one or two towns similarly encouraged. After the siege of Derry the city's arms were augmented by the arms of London and it became Londonderry. The royal tressure has been granted in Scotland both 'of grace' and 'of merit'.

7. Badges

Badges were in use before the advent of heraldry. They were devices with family or personal associations which identified the possessor and which in many cases formed the basis for later armorial designs. The badge often continued to be used for it had the advantages of simplicity and availability for use by servants, retainers and others claiming association with the owner but who could not display the arms. All sorts of household and military equipment carried the badge as well as clothes.

There was usually a reason for adopting a particular device — sentimental, political, commemorative, family association — and it was often more generally recognised than the arms. Some badges were personal and used exclusively by the owner while another badge served the household. A badge might appear intact in the arms and some were differenced or combined with others.

Until the twentieth century the most widespread use of badges was in the feudal period. The Wars of the Roses take their name from the badges of York and Lancaster, both white and red roses descending from the gold rose of Edward I. They were ultimately reunited by Henry VII to become the Tudor rose, which has ever since been a royal badge and the emblem of England. The thistle seems to have appeared later as a Scottish royal badge, certainly not as early as 1263, when a Danish invader at the battle of Largs is reputed to have betrayed an ambush by crying out when he stepped barefoot on a thistle — the traditional reason for its adoption as an emblem!

The red dragon of Cadwallader, emblem of Wales, has a pre-heraldic history as a British tribal emblem. Today's misnamed Prince of Wales feathers, the badge of the heir apparent, probably came from France. The Black Prince bore three black and silver ostrich feathers enscrolled *Ich dien*. Other Plantagenets used them, differencing by number, colour and arrangement. They became the special badge of the heir to the throne only in Tudor times.

Some badge devices figure in civic arms today through association with great landowners. The arms of Buckinghamshire County Council connect with the de Bohun and Mandeville families through the transmission of the swan badge by descent and marriage to the Staffords, Dukes of Buckingham. The famous bear and ragged staff badge of the Beauchamps, Earls of Warwick, passed to the Dudley earls and survives as a crest and charge in Warwickshire County Council's arms.

The Earls of Stafford bore as a badge (among several) a

Badges: (left to right, from top) Arthur Tudor, Prince of Wales; Heir-apparent; England; Scotland; shamrock of Ireland; harp of Ireland; Anjou (planta genista); Wales, Buckinghamshire; Mary Tudor; Warwick-shire; Stafford knot; Dacre knot; Lacy knot.

knot of intertwined cords, appropriated now as a favourite charge in civic arms in Staffordshire. This 'Stafford Knot' is quite different from several other forms all used as badges: the Harrington knot is hardly one at all, nor the badges of Lord Dacre and the Lacys.

While an armiger may apply for a badge and license its use, it is personal and quite different from the badges of the impersonal bodies which have proliferated in recent years, many of which have no heraldic background. On the other hand, civic authorities and corporations with arms may obtain badges for use by subsidiary bodies and societies not entitled to use the arms.

The armed forces use some of their badges with the original intention of immediate recognition. Many army badges are heraldic in origin and are successors to the medieval retainer marks. In 1918 the Royal Navy found that it had to rationalise unofficial adoption of badges for ships and conformed to an heraldic standard, incorporating elements of royal heraldry with the advice of an Officer of Arms. Coming later to the scene, the Royal Air Force quickly accumulated a number of unofficial badges and in 1936 an inspector was appointed, again an Officer of Arms.

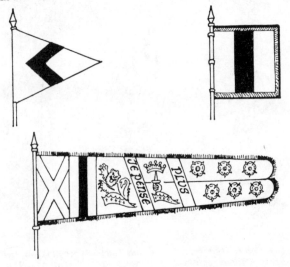

Upper left: pennon with chevron. Upper right and lower: square banner and long standard.

8. Flags

Today any group wishing to identify itself may write its message on a large placard or banner to parade through the streets; associations of longer standing frequently adopt devices to use on badges, on banners or flags. The early trade unions and working men's associations had big embroidered banners like those used in Catholic countries on church festival days. Announcing an allegiance or association has taken this form since pre-heraldic days.

Heraldic ensigns were rather different because of the feudal society in which they were systematised; they were personally associated with an armiger while still providing a rallying point for a group by virtue of the feudal hierarchy. At the end of the thirteenth century three types of ensign were used, the pennon, banner and standard. The shape now recognised most widely as the flag is the banner.

A knight bore beneath the head of his lance a small triangular or swallow-tailed pennon, bearing his badge or a device from his shield, so that the charge was upright when the lance was horizontal. The standard was a flamboyant and much longer tapering shape which displayed a variety of devices, the livery colours and mottoes. It was a showpiece for festive occasions and did not display the arms as it does today. Now the arms lie next to the staff (in the hoist) with the badge and the motto on the fly.

The nobility and knights distinguished in battle could display their arms on oblong banners which were the military ensigns of those under their command. Later they descended the social scale and are used now by impersonal bodies bearing arms more often than by individuals.

The Royal 'Standard' is a banner, as is the Union Jack — a compounding of the national banners of England, Scotland and Ireland. The cross of St George and the saltire of St Andrew were combined in 1606 by James I, and the saltire of St Patrick was added in 1801. The banner of St George appears as a red cross with a white edge for the field; the banner of St Andrew is represented by the broad sections of white diagonal on the blue field; the banner of St Patrick is shown in the red diagonals on narrow strips of white diagonal for the field.

9. Civil and ecclesiastical heraldry

Feudal power depended on landowning, from the King at the top down to the lords of the manor, and the benefits of heraldry were enjoyed by landowners. As associations began to form in the lower ranks outside the system, for reasons of trade or common interest, they needed some degree of internal self-government and the King would be asked to recognise them and grant a charter conferring varying degrees of power. Leading townsmen, for example, needed to be able to influence local affairs and regulate trade; craft fraternities and traders required regulations to protect their standards. And ultimately such groups wished to display their corporate pride and status in heraldic style as recognition of their merit and dignity.

Although shields of arms are found earlier in seals, trade and craft guilds and some educational foundations were granted arms from the fifteenth century, towns and cities from the sixteenth century. As in personal heraldry, identification by an unmistakable mark in an illiterate age preceded or coincided with the adoption of official arms. This was also true of ecclesiastical arms, where bishops placed on their seals religious insignia which are often found in the arms assumed later.

Educational foundations — universities and their colleges and Eton College — were granted arms and later public institutions, such as the Royal Society founded by Charles II, were deemed eligible to bear arms.

Towns and cities have always tended to place in their arms devices representing aspects of their loyalties and interests. In early days charges associated with the King or the local lord or the sea are often found. In the nineteenth century towns developed rapidly with the growth of industry and subsequently gained greater autonomy in local government; as a result many more grants were made and these arms reflected more specifically the bases of the civic pride and prosperity. Whereas the mid-fourteenth-century arms of the City of London bear the red cross of St George and in the canton the sword of St Paul, Darlington's arms display the cross of the patron saint, Cuthbert, silver pallets representing the steel industry and in chief George Stephenson's locomotive. Kettering's shield bears a pelt representing the footwear trade and two fountains representing the Baptist Missionary Society, founded in the town. One of the supporters is a negro with a broken chain on his wrist, in honour of William Knibb, who worked for the abolition of slavery. In the arms of Berkshire the ancient white horse of Uffington has a pile hanging from

Kettering: sable a pelt or in chief a cross-crosslet fitchy of the last between two fountains each charged with a martlet of the first and for the crest on a wreath of the colours issuant from a circlet of chain flames proper; on the dexter side a griffin reguardant or beaked and membered and gorged with a chain reflexed over the back azure; and on the sinister side a negro proper habited about the waist with a cloth and his sinister wrist encircled with a handcuff pendant therefrom a broken chain azure.

its neck in punning reference to the atomic pile at Harwell.

Civic arms are very instructive in matters of local pride and sympathy. Parts of Kesteven, Lincolnshire, represents its Roman road, Ermine Street, with an ermine pale and has as supporters a Roman soldier and the Lincolnshire poacher. Parts of Lindsey incorporates the laurel wreath of Alfred, Lord Tennyson, the poet laureate. The crest of Wiltshire is the great bustard, representing the claim that the last one lived in the county, and Cambridgeshire makes the same claim and uses two as supporters. (The great bustard has returned to Wiltshire and is commemorated in the crest recently granted to West Wiltshire District Council, of a bustard resting a claw on a grenade.)

Lincolnshire, Parts of Kesteven: vert on a pale ermine, an oak tree eradicated proper; and for the crest on a wreath argent and vert a heron, in the beak a pike proper; the supporters following that is to say, on the dexter side a Roman legionary and on the sinister side a Lincolnshire poacher of the early nineteenth century both proper.

    The local government reorganisation of 1974 abolished urban, rural, city and borough councils and replaced them with district and parish councils. As the arms immediately became historic special provision was made for the possible transfer of arms where the jurisdiction and the name were more or less the same.

    Guilds and merchant companies similarly incorporated allusive and national insignia in their arms, such as the swords of the Cutlers, the arrows of the Fletchers, the barrels of the Vintners and the cloves of the Grocers (see *Discovering London's Guilds and Liveries*). They still have their livery colours, too, in direct line from the feudal use of distinctive colours for retainers.

Charges with ecclesiastical connotations include the crossed swords of St Paul, St Peter's keys, the mitre, the pastoral staff, the escallop of St James of Compostella and the pallium – a Y-shaped cross ending in a fringe. Thus the Province of Canterbury displays the silver staff of an archbishop topped with a cross paty, over which is a silver pallium fringed with gold bearing four black crosses.

City of London

Buckinghamshire

Spectacle Makers' Company of London

Vintners' Company of London

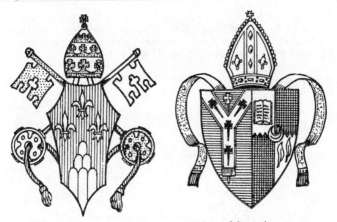

Ecclesiastical arms: a Pope and an Archbishop of Canterbury.

The unique attitude of the English to the established church is perhaps reflected in the way English clergy, excluding archbishops and diocesan bishops, have traditionally borne their personal arms like laymen, complete with helmet and crest. The Roman Catholic church evolved a system of tasselled hats to signify both calling and rank which recommended itself increasingly in recent years as a suitable option for Anglican clergy. At the request of the Archbishop of Canterbury, the Earl Marshal issued a warrant in 1976 authorising the use of appropriate hats from an approved list instead of crests. That of a deacon is black and untasselled, and that of a priest black with one black tassel either side with black and white cords; that of an archdeacon is black with three purple tassels either side with purple cords, and that of a dean black with three red tassels either side with purple cords. Only archbishops and diocesan bishops may impale their arms with those of their sees.

Most universities and colleges of later foundation have followed the older universities and obtained grants of arms. Most grants to public schools are comparatively recent, unlike Eton College, granted arms on its foundation in 1449. The BBC has its own arms and institutions of various kinds such as professional associations now bear arms. Even commercial companies, if sufficiently prominent and well established, have been granted arms since 1945.

The arms of the Commonwealth countries have an interest akin to that of civic arms, particularly those assigned most

British Broadcasting Corporation

Leeds University

Arms of Australia. The quarters represent the six states.

Arms of Tanganyika, 1961. The Tanganyikans are dressed in green and stand on a compartment representing Kilimanjaro. They support the native shield and elephant tusks.

recently. Their displays symbolise their history, development, resources or geographical location, tribal constitution and national aspirations. The charges used may be conventional or of traditional association but in recent years governments have drawn upon specifically non-European devices.

Canada's traditional display includes her emblem, the maple leaf, and the quartered coats of her original English, Scottish, Irish and French settlers, and their emblems. The emu and kangaroo support the Australian shield, which bears a shrike and the Southern Cross among other charges.

The more recently independent African states include some delightful achievements. Tanganyika was granted the first native shield in 1961 and was followed by Uganda and Kenya. Tanganyika and Uganda both display cotton and coffee bushes; Kenya and Uganda have crossed spears behind the shield. (Zanzibar has since joined Tanzania.) On a conventional shield the Gambia displays a Locar axe and a Mandinka hoe in saltire and the lion supporters each hold either the axe or the hoe. Trinidad and Tobago's arms feature 'three ships of the fleet of Christopher Columbus' and two hummingbirds.

10. Heraldry in other countries

Great Britain alone in Europe has provided a background sufficiently stable to ensure continuity in the line of heraldic officers and perpetuation of strict heraldic regulations. All the other nations have, to a greater or lesser extent, suffered shifting of frontiers, domination from outside, lack of internal unity and revolutionary change. Italian heraldry shows German, French and Spanish influence; Belgium has Spanish, French, and German designs. Swiss heraldry incorporates ideas from all the surrounding states. Nevertheless, there is usually a style or character to be discerned in shield, depiction of devices or associated emblems.

The three empires which dominated Austria and Germany from 962 to 1918 took the eagle, usually double-headed, as the imperial emblem; it was single-headed from 1871 and is so as used today by West Germany. Austria takes the eagle as the background for the shield. The arms of commoners often contain family ciphers. Several characteristically German crests bear the curved buffalo horns, reminiscent of Viking helmets but open and splayed at the tips. Anyone may assume arms, which then have limited legal protection. Civic arms are granted by state authorities.

The fleur-de-lis device of the French kings is perhaps the best known national emblem. Although it was abolished at the French revolution and replaced with the bee by Napoleon,

Above: West Germany. Left: buffalo horn crest. Right: Republic of Austria, 1945. Below: ciphers.

lilies abound still, particularly in civic heraldry. Crests and helmets had less importance in France than elsewhere and had largely disappeared by the eighteenth century (but have reappeared since) and nobility was indicated by coronets. Napoleon devised a standardised system of heraldry using caps to denote lower rank and robes of estate for higher ranks. It was wonderfully organised but lacked personality and distinction. Surprisingly little has remained. Arms may be freely assumed if they are novel and are protected by law.

Belgium has only been independent since 1831 and specifically Belgian arms are a recent development. Heraldic rules are strictly observed and are specific. Rank is indicated by helms and coronets and the highest ranks always bear supporters.

Noble arms are protected by law in Holland and are registered. Commoners have no protection and need not register but the use of arms is very widespread. There are no rules of composition of an achievement. Small saltires and martlets are popular devices, and so are rampant lions (as they are in Belgium).

Nearly every bourgeois and farming family in Switzerland seems to have a coat of arms as well as every parish and town — heraldry almost completely democratised. One striking feature in civic and cantonal heraldry is the simplicity of composition.

Spanish heraldry is recorded by heraldic registrars, Cronistas de Armas, and only registered arms can be publicly displayed. Grants are made by the King. The Spanish tradition has several distinctive features: white and silver, yellow and gold are not only used together but even one upon the other; elaborate bordures with castles, crosses, lilies, chains and even mottoes are common; where there is a coronet it is often placed on the shield and the helmet omitted as crests are rare. Grandees are entitled to a robe of estate.

The Portuguese nobility resented royal interference in armorial matters and rules of heraldry were not established until the sixteenth century. As it was always permissible to bear the arms of female ancestors there were more people entitled to bear arms and fewer grants than elsewhere. Thus a son, probably not the eldest, might choose from among his ancestral coats up to four to use, indicating by special marks of cadency and sometimes initials his relationship to the ancestor. Today anyone can assume arms but impersonal arms are carefully supervised.

It is surprising that Italian heraldry has any identity if unification a hundred years ago marked its beginning. But, while some characteristics predate unification, the heraldic

Left to right, from top: fifteenth-century arms of the Dauphin of France; Napoleonic pattern for a sovereign prince; Dutch arms, city of Bergen; arms of Switzerland; fifteenth-century Swiss craftsmen arms, tailor, carpenter; Spanish arms, city of Soria; arms of Portugal; Danish arms, city of Elsinore, fourteenth century.

authorities drew up their own system although allowing established elements of foreign systems to be incorporated. Strongly associated with Italy are almond-shaped and horse-head shaped shields. Titled nobility may set coronets on both shield and helm, and these may indicate two different ranks. Wreath and coronet are used together on the helm and, uniquely, the robe of estate of a prince or duke may be surmounted by a helm.

An interesting historical feature is the indication on the chief of a political allegiance — an eagle or eagle's head, black on yellow, indicating the Holy Roman Empire (Ghibellines) or three yellow fleurs-de-lis on a red label indicating the King of Naples, a branch of the French royal house (Guelphs). Civic heraldry is very plain, initials and simple charges being very common.

From left: Swedish arms, city of Stockholm, province of Scania; arms of Norway; Finnish arms, Pungalaitio; arms of Poland.

There was no distinction originally between noble and common arms in Denmark and the introduction in 1690 of crowns, helmets and quarters spoiled many ancient and dignified compositions. Interest in heraldry declined considerably until records of many medieval seals were resurrected by scholars. These were frequently adopted as basic devices for civic coats of arms. There were similar movements in Norway, Sweden and especially Finland. Where no ancient device was available new designs, identifiable by their modern emphasis on line and composition, have been adopted.

Communist countries have little to do with traditional heraldry beyond. establishing national arms and sectional emblems. Most Soviet states, satellites and communist republics have either based their arms on the Russian pattern or incorporated Soviet symbols with national ones. East Germany uses the roundel of wheat ears, but not the Soviet red star. Hungary uses both. Czechoslovakia and Bulgaria have retained as charges lions and Albania the double-headed eagle. Only Poland has kept, without the crown, its traditional coat. But there are many historic coats extant and, excepting personal and royal arms, perhaps they may be revived.

Coats of arms used in the United States of America often have strong European associations reflecting the countries of origin of immigrants. After independence a form of heraldry developed which, unlike the European systems, was unregulated and very symbolic and pictorial.

Left to right, from top: arms of Russia; arms of Czechoslovakia; arms of East Germany; Hungarian arms, city of Budapest; American arms of Dwight D. Eisenhower.

11. Royal heraldry

A citizen of the United Kingdom may have no idea what the arms of his local authority are but will recognise the Royal Arms and interpret the mottoes on the Garter and beneath the shield.

The three lions passant guardant came in with Richard I about 1198 and are referred to as *England*. While the claim to the French throne was maintained *France Ancient* (semē de lis) and later *France Modern* (three fleurs-de-lis) always appeared — it was not removed until 1801! On his accession in 1603 James VI and I incorporated the Royal Arms of Scotland — *or, a lion rampant within a double tressure flory counter-flory gules* — and the new arms of Ireland — *azure, a harp or stringed argent*. These elements, marshalled quarterly one and four England, two Scotland, three Ireland, have been the Royal Arms since 1837 when Queen Victoria succeeded and the Hanoverian arms were no longer included.

The Garter has usually encircled the shield since shortly after the institution of the order by Edward III. The *lion statant guardant or crowned proper* has surmounted the royal crown since the reign of Henry VIII and the motto *Dieu et mon*

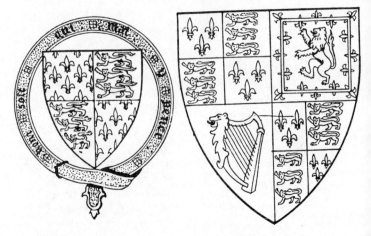

Left: royal arms of Edward III, 1340, showing the claim to France by quartering fleurs-de-lis. Right: royal arms of the Stuarts, 1603–88, incorporating Scotland and Ireland.

The royal arms. Quarterly, 1 and 4 England, 2 Scotland, 3 Ireland; the shield encircled with the Garter. Crest: upon the royal helm, the crown proper, thereon a lion statant guardant or, crowned proper. Mantling: gold lined with ermine. Supporters: dexter, a lion guardant or, crowned proper; sinister, a unicorn, armed, crined and unguled or, and gorged with a coronet of crosses paty and fleurs-de-lis, a chain affixed thereto passing between the forelegs and reflexed over the back, gold. Motto: Dieu et mon droit.

droit was fairly regularly used from Henry VI. Curiously our queens regnant have employed additional mottoes: Elizabeth I and Anne *Semper eadem* and Mary Tudor *Veritas temporis filia.*

Royal supporters changed from reign to reign and each monarch had his own personal and dynastic badges. The lion appears early as a supporter but the unicorn enters only in Stuart times to join it from then on. By then badges had reduced in number and consisted more or less of the national badges of today.

Above: white hart badge of Richard II. Left: portcullis badge of Beauforts and Tudors.

The Royal Arms of James VI and I as used in Scotland gave the Scottish arms precedence in the first quarter and this is still the practice. Similarly the crest is a lion *sejant affronty gules*; the motto *In defens* appears above; the supporters are reversed and hold banners, and the Order of the Thistle surrounds the shield. The royal Scottish motto *Nemo me impune lacessit* sometimes appears below.

The Royal Arms and badges are used by employees of the Crown — the crown appears on Post Office vans still and with the cipher on some post boxes — but most commonly in the coin of the realm. There has been some simplification since decimalisation but, except for Britannia on the 50 penny piece, all the obverse sides have an heraldic motif. The halfpenny bears the heraldic royal crown; the penny bears the portcullis of the Beauforts and Tudors, crowned; the 2 penny piece displays the badge and motto of the heir apparent (the Prince of Wales' feathers); the 5 penny piece, a crowned thistle; the 10 penny piece, a lion passant guardant (of England), crowned.

Royal arms as used in Scotland.

Seal of Thomas, Duke of Gloucester, 1395.

Officers of arms of the fifteenth and twentieth centuries. William of Bruges, first Garter King of Arms, 1420, wears the tabard or royal coat bearing the arms of Henry V on the front, back and sleeves and a gold crown. He carries a white staff. Today his crown, only worn at coronations, would be of silver gilt, crimson-lined, with tall serrated leaves rising from the rim, his baton of silver gilt and gold, surmounted by the imperial crown. The modern herald wears a satin tabard (velvet for Kings of Arms, damask silk for pursuivants) embroidered with the arms of the sovereign. The black velvet cap is worn at the Garter service and the staff of office is surmounted by a blue dove from the arms of the College of Arms. The collar of SS round his neck is of silver (silver-gilt for Kings of Arms) and bears the royal badge at the centre.

12. The heralds

By 1484, when Richard III incorporated the royal heralds as the Corporation of Kings, Heralds and Pursuivants of Arms and gave them their own headquarters, royal authority in armorial matters had been established for nearly a hundred years; the fount of power was also the fount of honour.

Since about 1260 there have been three ranks of herald: kings of arms, heralds and pursuivants. Garter King of Arms exercised general authority over the other kings and their subordinates. They performed most of the functions they undertake today in devising and granting arms and from the sixteenth century Kings of Arms were specifically empowered to do so. From the fifteenth to the seventeenth centuries heralds occasionally toured the country to check on the use of arms in practice. On such a visitation the officer made records and was empowered to confirm arms, destroy unlawful manifestations, require the appearance of offenders and cause the rectification or renunciation of pretended arms. Records of their investigations are preserved at the College of Arms.

Disputes were dealt with in the Court of Chivalry presided over by the Constable and Marshal (Earl Marshal since 1386), who became the chief officer of state representing the Sovereign, to whom the heralds were responsible. Their assistance at state ceremonies stemmed both from their original duties at tournaments and from their relationship to the chief organiser of state occasions, the Earl Marshal.

The Kings of Arms had territorial jurisdiction, as they have today. Clarenceux supervises south of the Trent, Norroy the north (including Ulster today). Lyon King of Arms in Scotland became independent and is still directly responsible to the monarch.

The number of heralds has varied, but the number and titles of the officers forming the Corporation of Royal Officers of Arms was fixed in 1555. There are thirteen Officers in Ordinary. Others can be appointed for ceremonial reasons, such as a coronation, but they are not members of the Corporation. They have always had distinctive titles, mostly reflecting the historic employment of heralds by barons; their names entered the royal service when they did. Today the heralds are Lancaster, Chester, Windsor, York, Somerset and Richmond.

The pursuivants were apprentices but now do much the same work as the heralds. Their names are Rouge Croix, Rouge Dragon, Portcullis and Bluemantle.

All officers of arms are created by Letters Patent. The corporation is now usually known as the College of Arms or Heralds' College and has been in Queen Victoria Street, London EC2, since 1555 although the original house was burnt down in the Great Fire of 1666. The records were saved, however, and the present building was erected. Here the officers deal with heraldry and genealogy, succession to titles and ceremonial. As members of the Royal Household they have a nominal salary but, as has always been the case, their main income comes from the fees they are allowed to charge, in early days mainly for ceremonial duties, then increasingly for the work of granting arms and advice as consultants. On ceremonial occasions they wear tabards with the Royal Arms on the back, front and sleeves. Heralds and Kings of Arms wear the collar of SS; the Kings of Arms have crowns to wear at coronations; Garter King, Lyon King and Norroy and Ulster have batons. All officers have their own badges and the Kings of Arms have official arms.

Today any individual or institution wishing to acquire arms applies to any of the heralds or pursuivants to prepare a memorial petition to the Earl Marshal that he will authorise, by warrant, the appropriate King of Arms to grant arms. Then a design is agreed by herald and petitioner and presented to the King of Arms, who judges it for uniqueness and heraldic acceptability. Letters Patent are prepared in which the design is painted on vellum by an heraldic artist, enrolled in the records, signed and sealed by Garter King and provincial King and given to the grantee. Grants always begin, 'To all and singular. . .'

To bear arms by inheritance, legitimate male descent from an armiger must be able to be established. In most cases there is no problem but where there are uncertainties the arms may be confirmed after enquiries by the heralds. They will also trace and record pedigrees.

Whereas in England there are remedies in civil law in the Court of Chivalry but not at common law for usurpation of arms and no necessary supervision of the family use and descent of arms, in Scotland there are penalties for using unregistered arms or infringing the owner's rights and only the heir male has a right to inherit them. Younger sons must matriculate with marks of cadency. Lord Lyon King of Arms and his heralds, Marchmont, Rothesay and Albany, and pursuivants, Ormond, Unicorn and Carrick, control a well regulated and logical system, with the Court of Lord Lyon as part of the Scottish legal system.

13. Evidence

The College of Arms possesses an unrivalled collection of heraldic material going back to 1264. It takes several forms, including compilations made by heralds of the arms within their areas, records of kings and the nobility, lists of the arms of participants in a battle and the records made by heralds on visitations. Rolls of Arms vary greatly in the manner in which they are drawn up and differ from the records of grants of arms which followed and took a more regular form. There are collections consisting of many thousands of bound volumes of manuscripts compiled by heralds now deceased and containing a wide variety of material. Ceremonials and detailed accounts of state ceremonies are preserved and there are printed books on all aspects of a herald's work. None are open to the public to consult.

But anyone may visit an old church and rarely will no heraldic designs be found there. Cathedrals often contain flags as well as inscribed tombs, tablets and windows, and many churches contain monuments in stone or brass bearing family arms.

Memorial brasses are particularly revealing as they provide finer detail than many monuments incised in stone — when the practice of engraving brass was introduced it was welcomed as an alternative to the laborious carving of expensive imported marble or stone. Heraldically aware generations coloured the plates, sometimes with enamel but more often with thick compounds, using lead or white metal for argent. As with other formerly vividly coloured church decorations few brasses retain any traces of colour nowadays.

From the earliest brass in England, that of Sir John d'Abernoun at Stoke D'Abernon in Surrey, to the late sixteenth century brasses show changing styles in costume and armour as well as coats of arms. Among the most interesting are those illustrating the corporate arms of the great merchant companies, found in the towns where they flourished.

Many churches possess the large sombre diamond-shaped panels called *hatchments* (the word is a colloquialisation of 'achievement'), which bear coats of arms. From the early seventeenth century it was the custom to hang a hatchment on the front of the house of a deceased armiger for the period of mourning and then to instal it in the church. The idea originated in the Low Countries and was adopted as an acceptable substitute for the declining custom of processing a knight's achievement (helm, shield etc) at his funeral.

As is usual in heraldry the hatchment told a full story.

Brasses of Sir Ralph Verney and his wife, Elizabeth, 1547, at Aldbury, Hertfordshire.

Usually made of wood or canvas stretched over a wooden frame, it carried the arms of the deceased and indicated by the background treatment his or her marital status. Where the dexter half of the lozenge was black and the sinister white, the husband had died, leaving a wife; where the colours were the reverse, the wife had died, leaving a husband. A completely black background behind a shield or lozenge indicated that a surviving spouse, bachelor or spinster had died. Where a man married twice the arms of his wives could appear as quarters on the sinister side, on either side of his own, palewise, side by side in the sinister half or as small hatchments in the angles of the panel. However it was done, the background behind the arms of the dead was always black.

The surrounding spaces often featured appropriate decoration, and cherubs' heads commonly took the place of the crest on a woman's hatchment. The words of the family motto might be replaced by a religious sentiment or hope such as *Resurgam* or *In coelo quies*. At the height of popularity at the turn of the eighteenth century they were draped in black crape. The custom is virtually extinct now.

Hatchments showing the deaths of (from left) a husband, wife, widow and widower.

Hatchments were not the only memorials in pictorial form. Many churches have commemorative armorial panels of other than lozenge shape. It was always expensive to commission a stone or brass monument and might be inappropriate. A family or grateful community might, therefore, have the arms painted on a board with a suitable inscription and display it in the church. The Royal Arms sometimes feature on armorial panels, installed as a mark of loyalty to the Crown.

The panel is commonly rectangular but a few are lozenge-shaped, particularly from the period before hatchments became established, and some have black and white backgrounds. Usually an inscription identifies an armorial panel and if that is absent the panel may have served as hatchment and memorial: clear-cut distinctions are the preoccupation of the historian, not of the participants.

Seals

Throughout this book it has been necessary to mention seals to illustrate features of early heraldry particularly and the sources of the later development of arms. Heraldic artists revelled in the scope offered by the shape and purpose of the seal to elaborate the principle of singularity and develop their art. They were engraved on many materials and were often double-sided, the two impressions forming the one seal. The Great Seals of England, for example, show on the seal the monarch on horseback, on the counter seal the monarch enthroned. Changes in the treatment of the figures and background reflect royal aspirations and contemporary taste in fashion, armour and architecture.

14. Identifying a coat of arms

There will be arms in churches and elsewhere which are not mentioned in immediately available literature. Usually it will be comparatively simple to identify the family from local sources and people, monuments in the church, gravestones, inn signs, the incumbent or the historical society. Should this fail the next stage is to record the arms in blazon, and perhaps roughly in trick, and note down likely names from the more impressive gravestones or local suggestions. Then visit the reference library. Look up the motto first in Fairbairn's *Crests of the Families of Great Britain and Ireland* or Elvin's *Book of Mottoes*. Likely names can be checked in Burke's *General Armory*, which lists arms under family names alphabetically (but which ought to be used carefully as it is not entirely authoritative). Either as a check or initial identification the actual charges can be looked up in Papworth's *Ordinary of British Armorials*, where charges are listed alphabetically, but in blazon. Crests can often be located in Fairbairn.

The actual person who bore the arms may perhaps be identifiable through the parish register if he lived locally or in Whitmore's *A Genealogical Guide* or Marshall's *The Genealogist's Guide,* again alphabetically organised in families. (This can take a deal of persistence.)

Seal of Henry of Lancaster.

Further reading

Brooke-Little, J.P. *Boutell's Heraldry*. Warne, revised edition 1979.

Brooke-Little, J.P. *An Heraldic Alphabet*. Macdonald, second edition 1975.

Brooke-Little, J.P. *Royal Heraldry: Beasts and Badges of Britain*.

Child, Heather. *Heraldic Design*. G. Bell, 1965.

Cook, Malcolm. *Discovering Brasses and Brassrubbing*. Shire Publications, seventh edition 1976.

Fox-Davies, A.C. (revised by J.P. Brooke-Little). *A Complete Guide to Heraldry*. Nelson, 1969.

Franklyn, J. and Tanner, J. *An Encyclopaedic Dictionary of Heraldry*. Pergamon Press, 1974.

Hope, W. St John (revised by A.R. Wagner). *A Grammar of English Heraldry*. 1953.

Innes of Learny, Sir Thomas (revised by Malcolm Innes of Edingight). *Scots Heraldry*.

Moncrieffe, Ian and Pottinger, Don. *Simple Heraldry*. Pilgrim Press, 1977.

Neubecker, Ottfried. *Heraldry*. McGraw-Hill, 1975.

Summers, Peter G. *How to Read a Coat of Arms*. National Council of Social Service.

Von Volborth, Carl Alexander. *Heraldry of the World*. Blandford, 1973.

Wagner, A.R. *Heralds of England*. HMSO, 1967.

Wagner, A.R. *Historic Heraldry*. Phillimore, 1972.

Pamphlets and other publications of the Heraldry Society. List available from the Secretary, the Heraldry Society, 28 Museum Street, London WC1A 1LA.

Index